What Happened To Honor?

Doing Right in Ministry and Life

Joel Siegel

What Happened To Honor?
ISBN 978-0-9888535-2-2
©2013 Big God Media / Siegel Ministries, Inc

Dedicated to People of Honor

It's amazing how infectious honor is. If you spend much time around it, it will work its way into the deepest parts of your being and stay there forever.

I have lived a life of privilege, in that I have been repeatedly exposed to the characteristics of the honorable life. This began early for me, having been raised in a home with honorable parents. I am fortunate also to have a wife and close friends who are committed to the life of honor.

There have been others as well, men of honor and true greatness who (along with their equally honorable wives) were brought into my life at certain seasons, strategically placed by God for my development. It is to these men – my fathers and mentors – that I wish to dedicate this book:

Dr. Roger Breland gave me my first position in ministry, and saw things in me that I didn't see in myself. Though he stood on stage in front of thousands, I also observed his private life, and saw how a Christian should live. From him I learned how a man of God stays in the Word, treats his wife and kids, and regardless of the circumstances just keeps showing up.

Rev. Kenneth E. Hagin was my spiritual father, a man I traveled with for several years. Known to many as the father of the faith message, I also knew him to be skillful with the love of God. Watching his life was watching love and honor in action. From him I learned the integrity of God's Word, the flow of God's power, and that *putting the other fellow's candle out won't brighten yours any.*

Rev. Kenneth W. Hagin, my pastor for many years, has spent his life fulfilling the vision that began with his Dad. It would move me to see Rev. Hagin express love and respect for his father, and I watched as he selflessly shared him with the world. Pastor Hagin has trained thousands for ministry, and has believed in people when others wouldn't.

Dr. Ed Dufresne is a man who has given honor the lead position in his life and ministry. Deeply committed to the call of God, he is faithfully helping to lead the body of Christ into its greatest day. A man of compassion, skill, and greatness, he generously allows others to partake of the anointing on his life, and is gifted in helping ministers reach their potential. I am proud to be associated with him.

CONTENTS

Honor In Life

APPENDIX
Pastors And Traveling Ministers

Introduction

This is not a book I would necessarily choose to write, but rather one I feel compelled to write because of some things I know about God, the devil, and people. I *know* there is a move of the Spirit of God that is imminent and necessary, but is yet in jeopardy. I know the devil is as focused and committed as ever as he tries to halt the plans that God has for the earth. And I know that people are searching for truth, hungry for answers and results, and desirous that the will of God be done.

God wants to do great and mighty things in our midst that He presently cannot; He is limited by our cooperation and participation. Because His work on earth cannot be accomplished apart from His Body, it is essential that the Church stay awake and focused. Time is too short for distractions and wrong directions. Time is too precious to present poor substitutes for the real power of God. In the past, the Body of Christ has experienced great demonstrations of the Spirit of God, and has been the recipient of some of the finest teaching the world has ever known. These things were not just passing fads; the precious things that we have received must not be abandoned.

Throughout this book, I make reference to a man by the name of Rev. Kenneth E. Hagin. I consider "Dad" Hagin (as he was fondly called) to be my spiritual father, for, more than any other person, he trained me in the ways of God. Brother Hagin spoke prophetically about the great move of God which must precede the Return of Christ, emphasizing the place of reverence and honor. I have heard him say, "When these things (reverence and honor) are restored, there will be a restoration *and a multiplication* of the miraculous power of God." It is with a sense of passion, and even desperation, that I humbly add my voice to his, calling for the restoration of a culture of honor within the Church.

The move of God and plan of God require the honor of God. The problem in our day is a lack of honor that is eroding the effectiveness of the Church and limiting the power of God. Perhaps an even bigger problem is that the whole process seems to be going unnoticed by many ministers and leaders.

What I've seen the Church literally throw in the trash in recent years scares me. Things that should have been hallowed forever are being called old and obsolete. People who think they are doing the Body of Christ a great service are encouraging leaders to leave behind the *old* and embrace the *new*. The result is a Church that is powerless, faithless, and honor-less.

I believe that many consider the subject of honor to be of great importance. What we may not all be clear on however, is what honor looks like and how it acts. The chapters that follow will attempt to bring scriptural definition to the honor of God. Although I plainly speak of certain pitfalls and errors, my intent is not to present a negative message. This is a book borne out of love. I am persuaded that as the Church pursues honor – a trait that mirrors the very essence of God – He will move in His fulness, and the Church will enjoy its greatest day.

THE
HONOR
CRISIS

CHAPTER 1

"Don't Drink The Kool-Aid"
Embracing The Right Kind Of Change

But test everything; hold fast what is good.
1 Thessalonians 5:21

Honor has been on the decline for years, as the church world has embarked on what can only be described as a fast-paced race to the bottom. It sometimes seems like a competition to see who can embrace more of the values and standards of the world while still bearing the name of Christ.

Every day, more congregations jump into this race. Their spiritual leaders are telling them that unless sweeping change in the order of worship takes place they will not be *relevant*, and therefore will not reach people. That is not necessarily true.

The concept of change is certainly scriptural, but not all change is good change. Good, godly change always leads to one

3

place: Christ-likeness. The Church has had its share of change in recent years, but so much of that change has conformed the Church into the image and likeness of the world instead of into the image of Christ.

> *And we all, with unveiled face, **beholding the glory of the Lord, are being transformed into the same image from one degree of glory to another.** For this comes from the Lord who is the Spirit.*
>
> *2 Corinthians 3:18*

When we move with God, His glory manifests in a variety of ways. As we experience and behold the manifestation of His glory, we are changed into His image – full of His glory. We actually become what we behold, and are to progress from one degree of His glory to higher degrees of glory. This is the pattern for growth and development that every church should pursue, until our congregations look no different than Jesus' ministry on earth.

Leaders today however, have been implementing change that has diminished the work of the Spirit and the manifestation of His glory. In its most radical forms, these changes have made the Church indistinguishable from the world. In some cases, there is more immorality in the local church than in the world. I have seen towns where the values of those *not* in church appear to be higher than those in the church.

This race to the bottom needs to come to a screeching halt. The turnaround starts when we recognize that in many cases truth has been mixed with error. The things we do in our worship services still look like truth and sound mostly like truth, but they have been tainted just enough to lead us down a wrong path.

Many years ago, a cult leader convinced approximately 900 of his people to drink flavored water that was mixed with poison. It is from this tragic event that we get the phrase, "Don't drink the Kool-Aid." Many are familiar with this event, but all might not know that this mass suicide was staged and rehearsed by the cult followers and leaders a few times before it actually took place. They were given the drink each time, not knowing whether the poison was included. When the poison was finally mixed in, there was no distinct poison flavor. It tasted just like the grape juice they were used to, but with lethal effects.

Some of the change occurring in the Church in our day is poisoning our Kool-Aid, spiritually speaking. The purity of our faith is being compromised, and as a result, some of the precious things of God are slowly being killed off. It may not be anyone's intention to taint the move of God, but it is happening nonetheless.

> *Now about spiritual gifts, brothers, I do not want you to be ignorant.*
>
> *1 Corinthians 12:1 (NIV)*

The things of God that are being compromised are *spiritual* things. When we speak of the things of the Spirit, we are referring to a broad array of supernatural happenings, such as healing and miracles; flows of prayer, praise, and worship; ministers speaking by divine revelation, and so on. These manifestations of God's presence and power require a degree of understanding and cooperation if we are to benefit from them. Where ignorance exists, the manifestation of the Spirit is usually absent.

Some of the "how we worship" decisions being made in churches reflect a great deal of spiritual ignorance. These decisions (in most cases designed to attract new attendees) are hindering the flow of God instead of catering to it. As a result, Christians incorrectly believe that we are waiting for God to move – to "send His power" – when it is really *He* that is waiting for us to learn His ways. Some think that the true manifestation of God is happening in their services, but in many cases it is really just a demonstration of natural excitement, fueled more by the flesh than by the anointing.

We find ourselves in error in the local church when we focus too much on people (their likes and dislikes) and not enough on the Lord. Services in many churches today are produced like TV shows where people only have to show up and watch. Provision is not made for the movement of God. There's nothing wrong with wanting the people who visit and attend our churches to feel comfortable, but when their comfort is our *pri-*

mary concern, the spiritual climate will be compromised, and we will experience less of the supernatural.

When leaders are eagerly looking to fill the seats in their churches, they often accept the first idea that comes along that looks good. Please, let's stop and examine what we're doing to make sure we're not hindering the movement of God in our midst. We all want success, but we are not to just blindly move in the direction that's popular. The results of wrong movement may not be seen right away, but there will eventually come an unwanted harvest. The change that was supposed to make things better can end up making things worse. We don't want the drink that was supposed to refresh us to end up poisoning us.

CHAPTER 2

Following Success

We must choose carefully which voices we listen to. Just because a person sells a lot of books or is on television does not make them correct. And, just because someone once had a ministry that was approved of God does not mean that his or her present direction and message is on course. We must examine things in the light of the Word of God, being careful to use only God's standard of measurement.

REAL SUCCESS

*You did not choose me, but I chose you and **appointed you to go and bear fruit** – fruit that will last. . . .*

John 15:16 (NIV)

The world measures success based on how large an enterprise has become. The companies that are the most popular, far-reaching, and the largest of their kind are the ones the world calls most successful, and rightfully so. However, we cannot apply that same standard to the Church, because the Church is not just a worldly enterprise. First and foremost, the Church is a spiritual organization. Its success is not measured simply in the natural, but in the spirit-realm where only God has complete clarity of sight.

The most successful church or ministry is not necessarily the largest, but the one which has the greatest *spiritual* impact. Not just the strongest numbers, but the most anointing and fruit. Using God's measuring stick, we see that a relatively small church can supersede the mega-church in spiritual impact, and therefore is more successful. All of us (God included) would like large numbers, inasmuch as it means more people being reached with the gospel, but never do numbers alone mean that we have been successful. We must adopt God's measure for success and stop looking at things solely from the world's point of view.

There are many large churches that have no spiritual depth. They are like tall trees with no roots, or a building with no foundation. Everyone thinks they are successful because of their new youth facility or café, but if those churches don't learn to honor the Word and flow with the Spirit, they will eventually fail. Often, these kinds of churches are following man's business models instead of God's plan. Here are a few of the several scriptures that speak to this:

> *Unless the LORD builds the house, those who build it labor in vain. Unless the LORD watches over the city, the watchman stays awake in vain.*
>
> *Psalm 127:1*

> *And everyone who hears these words of mine and does not do them will be like a foolish man who **built his house on the sand**. And the rain fell, and the floods came, and the winds blew and beat against that house, and it fell, and great was the fall of it.*
>
> *Matthew 7:26-27*

Failure to understand God's definition of success is a big problem among those in spiritual leadership. Ministers continue to pursue what they think is a formula for success, while unknowingly forsaking the elements that bring true success: *the things of the Spirit.* We must be careful to not follow leaders just because they appear successful by worldly standards. They may not be a picture of true spiritual success.

Here's a tip to help all of us identify the kind of spiritual leaders that are worth following: *look for the anointing.* That is

God's stamp of approval. Seek the Lord and make sure it is He who is drawing you to a minister or ministry, not just your own personal desire. When we find and follow true spiritual success, we will ourselves experience success.

CHAPTER 3

Losing The Landmarks

Do not move the ancient landmark that
your fathers have set.
Proverbs 22:28

K*eep in place that which your fathers have set in place.* This concept contradicts the thinking of today's culture, and today's Church. Society trends toward forgetting our past rather than embracing it. This wrong way of thinking is programmed into people when they are taught evolution instead of creation. Evolution thinks that everything is progressing, getting better all the time. If it's true that everything is better this year than it was last year, then there's not much reason to look back and cherish anything old, is there?

The Bible shows a different progression. God created everything to be perfect, and society has steadily devolved from there. Sure, technology continues to progress, but the effects of sin and Satan on the earth and humanity keep society on a downward course, slowed only by those in the Church that allow the light of the Gospel to fully shine.

It doesn't take an ivy-league degree to see that things in the world aren't on the right track. Common sense and the Word of God both teach us to take a look back to the days when things worked better, and learn the secrets to success. Find out who did it right, see why it worked, and follow the same pattern. Yes, as has been said, technology is different, and information may flow differently, but human beings are the same, and God is the same.

WHAT IS A LANDMARK?

We don't use the term *landmark* much in our day, but everyone is familiar with road signs. Signs along the roadway let us know where we presently are, and point us to where we want to go. When at a crossroads, we often find signs pointing in every direction. If you want to avoid a particular section of town, follow the signs that show you another way. Signs, or landmarks, are fixed points that help us navigate through life. They are reminders of where we have been, and predictors of future direction.

I don't want to be a person who drives along a road paying no attention to the signs. That's a sure way to get off-course.

Many people spend their whole lives wandering around in such a fashion. They stubbornly insist on making every decision for themselves, free from the counsel of others. You may enjoy making all of your own mistakes, but I prefer to learn from the mistakes of others, avoiding some of the trial and error that they went through. Listen to what our fathers in the faith are teaching us. Very often, their words to us are the landmarks we are to follow. If we will look at their lives (following their faith), we can have their results.

> *"Listen to me, all you who are serious about right living and committed to seeking GOD.* **Ponder the rock from which you were cut, the quarry from which you were dug.** *Yes, ponder Abraham, your father, and Sarah, who bore you. Think of it! One solitary man when I called him, but once I blessed him, he multiplied."*
>
> *Isaiah 51:1-2 (MSG)*

GODLY LEADERS HAVE NO EXPIRATION DATE

Oh, oh, oh... How gold is treated like dirt, the finest gold thrown out with the garbage, priceless jewels scattered all over, jewels loose in the gutters. And the people of Zion, once prized, far surpassing their weight in gold, are now treated like cheap pottery, like everyday pots and bowls mass-produced by a potter.

Lamentations 4:1-2 (MSG)

We love to get something new and throw out the old. I understand that the new is exciting, and I enjoy new things as much as anyone. But when we start to throw out our godly leaders, something's wrong, and that something is a lack of honor.

When did we decide that it was okay to discard a man or woman of God because he or she is older? Their longevity gives them valuable experience and insight that cannot be gained any other way. Worldly marketing strategies may suggest that a younger face is necessary to move an organization forward, but why are we applying these kinds of standards to the Church? People seem to believe that the older a person is, the less they know. That really makes no sense. Sadly, this kind of logic has always been prevalent.

And Jeroboam and all Israel came and said to Rehoboam, "Your father made our yoke heavy. Now therefore lighten the hard service of your father and his heavy yoke on us, and we will serve you." He said to them, "Come to me again in three days." So the people went away.

Then King Rehoboam took counsel with the old men, who had stood before Solomon his father while he was yet alive, saying, "How do you advise me to answer this people?" And they said to him, "If you will be good to this people and please them and speak good words to them, then they will be your servants forever." **But he abandoned the counsel that the old men gave him, and took counsel with the young men who had grown up with him and stood before him.** *And he said to them, "What do you advise that we answer this people who have said to me, 'Lighten the yoke that your father put on us'?" And the young men who had grown up with him said to him, "Thus shall you speak to the people who said to you, 'Your father made our yoke heavy, but you lighten it for us'; thus shall you say to them, 'My little finger is thicker than my father's thighs. And now, whereas my father laid on you a heavy yoke, I will add to your yoke. My father disciplined you with whips, but I will discipline you with scorpions.'" So Jeroboam and all the people came to Rehoboam the third day, as the king said, "Come to me again the third day." And the king answered them harshly; and* **forsaking the counsel of the old men, King Rehoboam spoke to them according to the counsel of the young men,** *saying, "My father made your yoke heavy, but I will add to it. My father disciplined you with whips, but I will discipline you with scorpions."*

2 Chronicles 10:3-14

Rehoboam was given charge of the most blessed kingdom the world has ever known. It was blessed largely because of the obedience and honor of his father, Solomon, and grandfather, David. Rehoboam obviously hadn't learned some of the principles that brought his elders success. To him, the voice of the younger generation spoke loudest; they represented the future. They may be the future, but that doesn't mean they have any wisdom whatsoever.

Though Rehoboam did seek the advice of his elders, it's possible that he checked in with them only as a courtesy, having no real intention of taking their advice. Many today do likewise, but grave consequences often follow. In King Rehoboam's case, failure to follow voices of wisdom and experience caused the greatest kingdom on earth to become a divided kingdom.

> *So Israel has been in rebellion against the house of David to this day.*
>
>

2 Chronicles 10:19

IT GETS WORSE

Rehoboam also presided over another leadership disaster. His once-great kingdom, now weakened, became a target for his enemies, who began to attack. On one occasion, the gold articles from the house of God were stolen. Gold in the house of God represents purity of heart and worship. Notice how Rehoboam tried to compensate for this loss:

*He took away the treasures of the house of the Lord and the treasures of the king's house. He took away every-thing. He also took away all the shields of gold that Sol-omon had made, and **King Rehoboam made in their place shields of bronze**, and committed them to the hands of the officers of the guard, who kept the door of the king's house.*

1 Kings 14:26-27

When landmarks (fixed points) are not in place, it's easy to bring in poor substitutes for the real things of God. By sub-stituting the mixed alloy of bronze for the purity of gold, Re-hoboam compromised what God had ordained for the temple, and didn't see anything wrong with it. He didn't see, because he wasn't in the habit of looking back. In similar fashion, many forward thinking people today are substituting the brass of the flesh for the pure gold of true worship. We must *contend for the faith that was once for all delivered to the saints* (Jude 1:3), and steer clear of the failures of King Rehoboam. [For a more detailed study of this subject, see Rev. Kenneth E. Hagin's book *Plans, Purposes, and Pursuits*.]

Some time later, a king rose to power who learned that in some respects the way forward is to look back. God was able to add His blessing to the efforts of that king, and the people experienced great increase as a result.

The Lord was with Jehoshaphat, because he walked in the earlier ways of his father David . . . .

2 Chronicles 17:3

Those looking for success in the future will always benefit from a look back to the successes of the past. When a younger person is in leadership, he or she is wise to surround himself with godly elders and heed their counsel. The guidance of seasoned elders helped the young pastor, Timothy, to successfully lead the church at Ephesus. Likewise, those in our era who have preceded us should be honored as a valuable resource.

CHAPTER 4

Recognizing Greatness

*The one who receives a prophet because he is a proph-
et will receive a prophet's reward, and the one who
receives a righteous person because he is a
righteous person will receive a
righteous person's reward.*
Matthew 10:41

One of my spiritual mentors often comments that a quality lacking in Christians today is the ability to recognize
greatness in others, young or old. We live in such conscious-
ness of the natural realm, living based on what we physically
see, that we often don't perceive what is in a person. When we
fail to recognize great people, we miss great things.

I am reminded how, in the Star Wars saga, Luke Skywalker
initially discounted everything the elder Obi-wan Kenobi told

him, only later understanding that he had been in the presence of greatness. He had to deal with competing voices that were telling him that the seasoned warrior was just a senile old man who wasn't culturally relevant. Again, when Luke first met Jedi Master Yoda, he thought Yoda was just an eccentric old frog. He failed to see the greatness within Master Yoda because he was confused as to what greatness looked like. He didn't realize until much later that someone who had been training warriors for 900 years might still know a thing or two.

Like Luke Skywalker, Christians can find themselves in the presence of a person of greatness and be completely unaware of it. The greatest man ever to walk on our earth was the Lord Jesus, and to a large degree, His greatness went unrecognized in His day. When people fail to recognize greatness, not only do they miss a personal impartation into their lives, they subject themselves to the attacks of the enemy. The encounter with greatness that they missed was their safety and help in time of trouble.

And when he drew near and saw the city, he wept over it, saying, "Would that you, even you, had known on this day the things that make for peace! But now they are hidden from your eyes. For the days will come upon you, when your enemies will set up a barricade around you and surround you and hem you in on every side and tear you down to the ground, you and your chil-

*dren within you. And they will not leave one stone upon another in you, **because you did not know the time of your visitation.***"

We must take care not to overlook the times of visitation that God has prearranged for our good. Don't argue with the truth you hear, but respect the answers of our elders and hold their words closely. Thank God, even the most dishonorable person can learn to recognize and respect greatness, and begin to reap positive benefits. In young Master Skywalker's life, it wasn't long until he began to see what his fathers were trying to teach him. He eventually saw that The Force that they spoke of was his most precious commodity.

BECOMING A GOOD STUDENT

As a young man, I seemed to excel as a jazz performer. I was blessed with some of the best musical instruction available anywhere, and it benefitted me greatly. One summer, I was invited to be part of a select group of players that got to spend the day at the home of a world-famous saxophonist. This great player could no doubt sense the honor of the younger musicians present, so he began to impart some of his knowledge and experience into our lives. As we all descended the staircase into his basement music room, he taught us how to be not only good musicians, but how to be good students, for the good musician is always learning. He made two statements on that staircase that have stayed with me over the years. The first was this: "When you get to visit with a great musician, there are only two questions to ask: 'What books? What records?'" To this day, when at the home of a respected man or woman of God, I always try to sneak a look at their bookshelf.

He was trying to teach us that one of the best ways to glean from a person who has attained success is to ask them to point you to the source of their knowledge.

The second statement he made amplified the first: "When you get to study with someone great, first get familiar with their books and recordings, so you don't waste their time asking things you should already know." In other words, realize who you are with, be a good student, and treat them with the honor that their place deserves. This musical icon taught us all that greatness must be recognized and respected if we are to enjoy an audience with it. I have had many opportunities to apply his valuable advice.

When I began making the transition from full-time jazz musician to full-time ministry, I enrolled in RHEMA Bible Training College, a Bible school founded by Rev. Kenneth E. Hagin. From the time I applied, to the day school started, I spent all my free time listening to Brother Hagin's tapes and reading his books. I was new to his ministry and didn't want to be behind when I got to school. I crammed so much of his ministry into my heart, that I got to the place where I could tell all his stories along with him. I was bringing honor to the opportunity that was before me.

The honor I brought to my ministry training was later rewarded as I was invited to travel with Brother Hagin to all his crusade meetings. I saw and received things that forever changed my life. I could tell many inspiring stories of the miraculous move of God that I experienced during my time with Brother Hagin. It's amazing to me that very few people show any interest in hearing those stories.

Just like a trained chef has developed his sense of taste until he can discern the slightest variation of seasoning in a recipe, we must develop our spiritual senses until we can easily recognize the presence of a person of greatness. Only then will we bring appropriate honor, receiving great impartations from our times of visitation.

CHAPTER 5

Spiritual Fathers

Children, obey your parents in the Lord, for this is
right. "Honor your father and mother" (this is the first
commandment with a promise), "that it may go well
with you and that you may live long in the land."
Ephesians 6:1-3

I understand that the verses above are speaking primarily of the natural parent-child relationship, but I believe it is also appropriate to make a spiritual application. If we will honor those who are our spiritual *parents* (leaders), it will go well with us. I have proven this verse true in my life many times. When I have failed to show proper honor to those the Lord has placed over me, there have been negative effects. When I have shown honor, things have gone well.

My biggest influence in the things of God was (and continues to be) a man named Rev. Kenneth E. Hagin. Although disregarded by a large part of the Christian community, many nevertheless knew him as a person of true greatness. As I spent years traveling with him, I observed that greatness in both public and private settings. I can think of no one else in recent history whose ministry has been as far-reaching or fruitful.

Brother Hagin lived a long time and ministered until the time of his death. I sometimes listen to the recordings of his last crusade meeting and am amazed at how sharp he was, spiritually and mentally, at an age when many people would just be occupying a rocker. His Bible School has tens of thousands of graduates, and countless ministers owe their success to him.

As I traveled on the road with Brother Hagin, it would grieve me that so few of the ministers he trained would take time to attend the meetings when we were in their area. Although his abilities to minister weren't slipping at all, I noticed that during the last few years of his life his crowds were slipping. People began to listen to other voices because they were enamored by something they thought was new.

Since Brother Hagin went home to be with the Lord, his followers have left him en masse. God had led him over the years to take steps to ensure that his ministry would survive him. Dozens of book titles were published, and hundreds of recordings of his services still exist today. He always taught the same truths year after year, because he stuck with the Word of God, and the Word never changes. In what he taught, what he did, and how he lived, Brother Hagin left many landmarks for the rest of us to follow.

As I travel throughout the Body of Christ and observe many of the works that his ministry influenced, I am saddened at what I see. So many of the landmarks have been removed. Things he warned us not to do are being done by some of the people who once seemed closest to him. I personally know a pastor who, soon after Brother Hagin died, ordered that all his books be removed from his church's bookstore and all his sermon recordings be thrown in the trash. This was a minister who had previously testified that his whole ministry was a result of the irreplaceable things that Brother Hagin taught him. Then he threw it all away to follow a different style of ministry. What happened to honor?

A verse that we looked at earlier is worthy of repetition:

Oh, oh, oh... How gold is treated like dirt, the finest gold thrown out with the garbage.
                    Lamentations 4:1 (MSG)

Many other people, whether literally or symbolically, have done the same thing with the landmarks that great men like Brother Hagin left for them. They have bought the bill of goods that says that we need to move on from the old because God is doing something *new* today. Folks, when the Bible says the old is gone and the new has come (2 Corinthians 5:17), it's not talking about leaving the landmarks of truth that great men of God sacrificed to put into you! Truth *never* changes or goes out of style. God will never alter eternal truth to do something new.

STAYING WITH THOSE TO WHOM GOD HAS CONNECTED YOU

*Elijah said to him, "Elisha, please stay here, for the LORD has sent me to Jericho." But he said, "As the LORD lives, and as you yourself live, **I will not leave you.**" So they came to Jericho.*

2 Kings 2:4

*But Ruth said, "Do not urge me to leave you or to return from following you. **For where you go I will go,** and where you lodge I will lodge. Your people shall be my people, and your God my God.*

Ruth 1:16

It is wrong to call someone your spiritual father and then leave them, or leave that which they deposited in you. It's one of the most dishonorable things a believer can do. (If your leader has gotten into major error or sin that's a different story.)

Think about that main one whom God has used to impart into your life (maybe your pastor). In order for him or her to have developed to the place where God was able to use them to minister to you, they had to pay a price to learn some things. They had to be mentored themselves. How dare we count that price as insignificant? How dare we dishonor our fathers by abandoning those right things that they taught us? The price they paid to get truth to us ought not be in vain.

In the case of my spiritual father, Brother Hagin, I know some of what he went through to be able to get his revelation to me: walking eight miles each way to preach; being apart from his wife and kids ninety percent of the time; traveling to churches to preach where he spent more to get there than he received in the offering; sleeping in a chicken coop (true story); and many other uncomfortable situations. All these hardships worked to develop in him a rarely-found level of character, faith, and love. When I came along decades later, he imparted what he knew into my life.

I appreciate the price he paid, and refuse to slap him in the face, so to speak, by pretending that his ministry never happened. I will honor my spiritual father by being a good steward of what he put into me, and then walking on into even greater light.

"A son honors his father, and a slave his master. If I am a father, where is the honor due me? If I am a master, where is the respect due me?" says the LORD Almighty.

Malachi 1:6 (NIV)

The Church cannot move forward like it must until it reconnects to its past. I'm not talking about reintroducing the methods of the 1950's or even the 1990's; I'm speaking of nothing more than *reverently pursuing the revelation of the Word and the moving of the Spirit* that our fathers brought us. Have those things waned? Yes! To an enormous degree. Just like our culture has seen gradual decline over the decades, there has been a steady decline in the Church where all things spiritual are concerned, and most in the Body of Christ (and many in ministry) are unaware of it.

Can these areas experience a turn-around? Yes. Things can change dramatically in both the Church and the world. But, a shift in the culture of the world will never happen without the genuine move of God in the Church. We see the move of God only in a small measure today, but it's not because God isn't ready for more. A restoration of honor will unlock the reservoirs of the power of God, the Church will rise up in all its might, and the world will take notice with many coming into the fold as a result.

The Church is in need of strong, stable leadership today. I believe the leaders are there. They are the ones who have not removed the landmarks; the ones who have the faith to see what has worked, and stay with what they have been taught. We must honor them as they lead us forward in God.

CHAPTER 6

Casual Or Casualties?

And the voice came to him again a second time, What
God has cleansed and pronounced clean, do not you
*defile and profane by **regarding and calling***
***common and unhallowed** or unclean.*
Acts 10:15 (AMP)

The church seems to have lost its ability to distinguish between things that are special (holy or set apart) and things
that are common. We have allowed society to impose its ideals
on us, and they have taught us that everyone and everything
should be of equal importance. As a result, things and people
that should be revered and honored no longer are, and the
things of God, ministers of God, and even God Himself are not
treated as special and holy. We need help getting out of the pit

we have dug and fallen into, where everything and everyone is common and casual.

I have absolutely no problem being casual when the occasion is casual (going fishing or watching a football game, for instance.) What confuses me, is how we ever came to consider the worship of God a casual event. There ought to be *nothing* casual about worship. That's not to say that worship cannot be contemporary, relevant, fun, and even media-rich, to the degree that God is fully honored and the message is without compromise. Church ought to feel up-to-date rather than out-of-touch, but we go too far when a sense of casualness and commonness pervades the service.

In our quest to provide a worship experience that in every way resembles a rock concert, we have kept nothing sacred. People can come right from the nightclub into the church and barely notice a difference. The atmosphere is light and party-like. Entertainment and convenience have replaced anointing and substance. Leaders see the people's enthusiasm and think a move of God is taking place, when really so much of it is just a display of the flesh. Although it is not God's plan or desire, we find ourselves in the era of the casual church.

Of the many elements that comprise casual worship, the most obvious is casual clothing. Nothing says *common* like comfortable, casual clothes. I have nothing against casual clothing; I like my shorts, running suits, sweats, and jeans, and can be found wearing them when it's time to be casual. Worship is not one of those times.

There have been wars, small and great, fought amongst Christians when it comes to how to dress for worship. I'm not a fashion expert, but feel compelled to say some things along these lines. The prevailing thought in our day is that what we wear for worship doesn't matter. I disagree. I believe it matters, and it is an issue that goes way beyond just the clothes we wear. It is an issue of the heart, and it is an honor issue.

LEGALISM

People will usually nod in agreement when spiritual truths are being preached, but when you begin to talk about the outer man they cry out, "Legalism! Bondage!" This attitude might be traced back to days long ago when some churches were teaching extensively on dress and other lifestyle and behavioral issues. Their teaching may have originally come from the Spirit, but at some point it was taken to the extreme, crossing over into legalism and manipulation. How could you blame people who wanted to get out from under the kind of teaching that said a woman couldn't cut her hair or wear makeup, and if she did it was not just improper, she was in sin and would go to hell? Religious rule-making leaves as bad a taste in my mouth as it does in the mouths of others. Having said that, we must be openhearted, allowing God's Word, God's Spirit, and God's messengers to speak into every area of our lives.

There is a right kind of legalism. *Legal* has to do with things that pertain to the law. In the Kingdom of God, there are *spiritual laws* that must be cooperated with. We must obey the laws if we are to enjoy the benefits of the Kingdom. When we speak of things like dress, it's not that we are trying to impose our opinions on people, rob their individuality, or restrict their free choice; we are simply calling attention to spiritual laws because, like physical laws, spiritual laws work for everyone. Bringing honor to our worship by dressing appropriately is part of complying with God's spiritual laws, and that compliance will always produce a desirable result.

MAINTAINING BALANCE

With any Bible truth there is a balanced position in the middle of the road, and an extreme position on either side. Some of the same extreme teachings seem to pop up with each new generation, slightly modified to reflect changes in culture. For instance, many years ago some of the Pentecostal churches taught that it was a sin for a man to wear a necktie, especially one with bright colors. Decades later, as clothing styles changed, it became a sin *not* to wear a tie. Tie or no tie, the same error of extreme legalism was being taught. To stay balanced, we must find the spirit (not just the letter) of what God is saying, and apply it to our lives, in our present culture.

It's one thing to function within the culture of the world,

but it's another thing to *conform* to the culture of the world. We must not allow the world to impose its standards on the Church. The Church today has allowed modern culture to pull it into the ditch of extremism in the area of ultra-casual dress and appearance. We should actually be influencing society with our high standards of godliness, but have instead taken the lead in embracing all things casual. The holy occasion of worship is profaned when we regard it as common and casual.

Understanding Casualness

When we use terms like *casual, formal, business*, etc. we are not just speaking of standards of dress; the thought of the activities associated with those different levels of dress is also included. For example, if I am asked to wear business attire, I immediately think of *an important event* where business will be conducted. If I get to this event and the people I'm meeting have no agenda other than to sit around and chat, my first question is, "Why am I here, all dressed up?"

When I put the suit and tie on for what I thought was business, I not only dressed up for the occasion, my thoughts, attitude, and demeanor also became business-like. *What I was wearing helped to define everything about me at that moment.* Dressing up helps lift other parts of my life in an upward direction. Unfortunately, the opposite (dressing down) works the same way. Our dress can influence how we function.

The New "Sunday Best"

We should give proper consideration to what we look like, dressing appropriately for different occasions. Many remember the days when kids had school clothes, church clothes, and play clothes. You couldn't play in your school clothes because they were too nice. Your worship-wear was another level above that. Today it's all one-in-the-same: sloppy and casual. What we wear matters. We dress up for a wedding, not just to fit in, but because marriage (and the people marrying) are worthy of our respect. Some occasions (like weddings) demand a show of honor. The failure in our day to recognize worship as one of those occasions has become a Church-wide crisis.

Of course, we also can overly emphasize our external appearance, becoming showy and vain. Making church into a fashion show is the extreme on the other side of the road (see 1 Peter 3:3), and the Church world has, at times, fallen into that ditch. Clothing is by no means the whole substance of a person. It would be silly to think that the business suit could actually conduct business, or that a sporting uniform could win a ball game. That being said, clothing (and hair, makeup, etc.) is the most visible layer of a person, and can often reflect the inner layers of one's self.

THE OUTER MAN REFLECTS THE INNER MAN

We have been conditioned by society to believe that a person's outward appearance doesn't matter. Although Jesus did tell us not to wrongly judge, He also taught that we would know certain things about people by their *fruits*. Fruit is the visible, outer part of a person's life. I can't see the *root* of a tree to learn anything about it, but I can see the *fruit*. Likewise, I usually can't tell what's in a person until I see the outward product they present.

Just like the business suit represents more than a jacket and tie, being casual means so much more than the clothing choice of jeans and a hoodie sweatshirt. More than just a relaxed standard of dress, the casual revolution in our world reflects relaxed standards of living, with blurred boundaries across the board. Since casualness has always been associated with things that are less important, a casual lifestyle makes people feel okay about being careless with their money, loose in their sex life, relaxed toward their education, and indifferent toward those in authority, including God.

The transition to a casual society has not been the great achievement everyone thinks it is. I believe the negatives far outweigh the benefits of flip-flops over dress shoes. The answer to why our country has experienced a free-fall in academic achievement and overall excellence may be traced to the fact that we have become so casual.

DRESSING FOR SUCCESS

Although our culture has trended in the casual direction, by no means has dressing up for important occasions gone out of style. People who have an important place in society still dress up to show respect for their vocation. Journalists, who report the day's news, dress professionally. So do lawyers, financial executives, and elected officials. Professional athletes are often required to wear suits when traveling, and the hosts of late night TV all respect their place in the entertainment world by dressing for success. Stores need not worry; there is still sufficient demand for dress clothes by those in the world that recognize the importance of their place.

There is one institution, however, where things have changed radically. Evangelical churches across America are led and attended by people who often look like they just rolled out of bed. Casual pants and an un-tucked shirt have become the uniform for today's preachers. What a sharp contrast to those who coach basketball teams, where suits and ties are required. Are we to believe that basketball is a more important endeavor than representing God Almighty to the world? I know people are just following trends, but when trends fill our pulpits and seats with dishonor, they must be rejected.

CASUAL WITH THE WORD

By no means is the honor crisis in our day just a clothing issue. The overall sense of casualness has diluted worship until it is difficult to sense God in the service anymore. Also, the relaxed atmosphere has caused Christians to become casual with the Word of God. In many churches, no one even brings a Bible anymore. (That's because their hands are already full with coffee and breakfast sandwiches when they enter the sanctuary.) I rarely hear people talking about the Word with each other. Reverence and honor are missing because we are holding so strongly to our doctrine of casualness.

> *Therefore whoever **relaxes** one of the least of these commandments and teaches others to do the same will be called least in the kingdom of heaven.*
>
> *Matthew 5:19*

I was raised and educated as a Jew. One thing we learned was that the Word of God (the Torah, as we called it) was the most holy thing we had. Not only did you dress up to come hear it, the Word itself was dressed up. There was actually a ceremony during the service to remove the elaborate coverings that protected the Hebrew scrolls. Can you see the value in that? Is it any wonder that even though we are in the New Covenant, Old Testament saints like Abraham, Isaac, and Jacob, who brought honor to their worship, often got better results than the Church today?

> *So Jacob said to his household and to all who were with him, Get rid of the foreign gods you have with you, and purify yourselves and* **change your clothes**. *Then come, let us go up to Bethel, where I will build an altar to God...*
>
> *Genesis 35:2-3 (NIV)*

CHAPTER 7

Casual Or Casualties? — Part 2

Leaders, desperate for numerical church-growth, have gone overboard embracing casual worship, but their strategy has backfired. Our casualness has instead produced *casualties*: those who do not make it to the end of their race.

RELATING TO SINNERS

I'm fairly sure I understand the reason for the church-wide dress-down. I've always heard it explained that the purpose of casual dress in the church is to reach people and relate to them on their level. That sounds noble enough on the surface (and I'm all for reaching the lost), but follow that logic just a little deeper and there are big spiritual problems that are hard to reconcile.

To start with, casual dress gives the impression that the things of God are neither serious nor holy. Those of us who are aware that people's eternal destinies are at stake should consider the ministry of Christ too important to treat casually.

Many might argue that the reason they *do* dress down is because they are so concerned about the lost. I don't doubt their sincerity, but again, the logic just doesn't make sense. If I need a medical specialist, I am not turned off if he or she is dressed more formally than I. If I need a policeman, I don't mind that he's dressed up in a uniform. When receiving help from these professionals, it is actually a comfort to see them dressed in a way that shows they understand the importance of their place. I don't need a person wearing what I am wearing just so he or she can relate to me.

Why should the preacher or saint in a worship setting have to look like the sinner in order to reach them? I know Christians are trying to send the message, "Hey, we are all just like you," but that is not our message, nor is it true. The sinner is *not* one of us, and the Holy Spirit is working throughout the service to show him that, so that when the opportunity is presented, he will *become* one of us. When we gear our worship exclusively toward the comfort of sinners (the popular but less scriptural phrase in our day is the *un-churched*), we are actually working against the convicting ministry of the Spirit. Let's work on making God comfortable in our services, and we will have maximum effectiveness in preaching and demonstrating the good news of the love of Christ to the sinner.

We do of course, welcome the sinner as well as the saint into our services without casting a judgmental eye toward their appearance. We are not trying to lay down ritualistic law, nor are we advocating any form of snobbery, but are endeavoring to show a distinction between that which is common and casual, and that which is important and special. At all times we love all people, but above all else we love God and worship Him with our best.

THE MINISTER, THE ANOINTING, AND THE WARDROBE

When ministering and participating in worship services, different spiritual dynamics exist than those in our private devotional lives. Many do not understand some of the variables present in a worship setting. For example, in church, the pastor is not just a man; he is a man occupying a ministry office and is appointed and empowered by God. For the pastor's anointing to flow as it should, his place must be magnified and honored by both he and the congregation. One way the pastor can honor his office is by dressing in a worthy manner. Not a gaudy or ostentatious manner, but a respectful, worthy manner. An example of this is seen in the Old Testament when public worship was first organized:

Make sacred garments for your brother Aaron, to give him dignity and honor.

Exodus 28:2 (NIV)

The preacher is not the only one who must bring honor to worship. There is a corporate anointing that results when all who are present bring their worship and honor to God. This corporate anointing, when flowing strongly, will cause supernatural gifts to be manifested. When the people are ignorant of or unresponsive to the Spirit's work in this area, the supernatural power of God dissipates. The whole congregation must be taught to reverence and honor the invisible work of God that takes place throughout the service. Again, one way honor can be shown is by presenting ourselves appropriately when the occasion is worthy of our best.

The most outstanding feature of a worship service is the fact that God is personally present. His presence alone is worthy of a show of our highest honor and respect. When looking at how today's congregations worship, one wonders if the people are really aware of His presence at all. People do seem to know how to honor man when it is appropriate. We come to a funeral dressed reverently to show honor for a deceased person that really isn't even there. How much more should we reverence the real, tangible presence of God?

A RADICALLY DIFFERENT LIFE

Besides hindering the flow of God in a service, and obscuring the truth of God to sinners, casual worship also adversely affects the lives of believers. Believers in the casual church are not being shown how radically different their lives are to be. If Christianity is anything, it is a changed life, where we continually conform to the image of Christ. Am I to believe that this radical change affects every area of my life except my outward appearance? No way.

The Bible leaves no doubt that true spiritual transformation will affect every part of our lives. In his second letter to Timothy, Paul encourages us to lay aside our old standards in order to become *vessels of honor*. A vessel is a visible container that holds an object or substance. When we look at a vessel, we usually get a good idea of what's inside and can begin to form an opinion before we ever see the contents. That's why ladies usually get excited when they see a ring-sized box in a man's hand. Notice how this powerful passage in 2 Timothy reads in The Message Bible:

> *In a well-furnished kitchen there are not only crystal goblets and silver platters, but waste cans and compost buckets – some containers used to serve fine meals, others to take out the garbage. **Become the kind of con-***

> **tainer God can use** to present any and every kind of gift
> to his guests for their blessing.
>
> *2 Timothy 2:20-21 (MSG)*

At one time, we were all garbage cans (spiritually lost), but as born-again believers, the Lord considers us to be His fine china (the highest quality and standard.) Instead of being hidden under the sink, I am now out on display. My old life is non-existent; everything is new. I don't act the same, think the same, talk the same, or smell the same. I don't listen to the same music as the world. I can't justify sleeping with someone who is not my wife, or living with someone outside of marriage, as the world does. I don't drink what the world drinks, I don't watch the filth they watch, and I don't follow a worldly standard of dress.

Church is where my mind gets renewed to these truths. I go to church to see a bright picture of how different my life is supposed to be as compared to the world. It is a lie to believe that I have to be just like the world in order to reach the world. I can be as different from the world as light is from darkness, and if the power of God is allowed to flow, the world will see the light and a percentage of them will run to it. The nice, non-sloppy clothes that I wear to magnify and honor my Heavenly Father, and to respect the anointing on my life, will *never* keep anyone from knowing God. Compromise, lack of honor, and relaxed standards of living will keep many from seeing the light.

We've tried to reach people by becoming casual, but misrepresenting God is not the way to reach people. Because the Church looks just like the world, many in the church have gone back to the world – drifting far from the path because God's standards are not on display with clarity and accuracy.

I am not trying to dictate a specific, Church-wide dress code for worship, but rather encourage a high degree of honor that is born in our hearts and shown through our actions and our appearance. I'm not saying that God can never move where there is no necktie. That would be placing the emphasis on a piece of fabric instead of on the heart. I do believe that the fullness of the flow of God requires full honor from us. *If we want His best, we should bring our best.*

Honor
in
Ministry

CHAPTER 8

Honor In Ministry

*Pay to all what is owed to them: taxes to whom
taxes are owed, revenue to whom revenue is owed,
respect to whom respect is owed,*
honor to whom honor is owed.
Romans 13:7

Most people know quite well that taxes are not optional. At tax time, we must pay what we owe, whether convenient or not. In the same way, honor is not an option in our lives. The Bible speaks of honor being *owed*; it's an ongoing debt that is due daily. Honor must be ever-present in our lives, and must always be found in ministry; for it to be absent is unacceptable. Every day, we bring honor to God, to others who occupy places of ministry, and to our own calling and ministry.

Honor has to do with having the right heart and doing the right thing. More than just an inner quality, honor reaches into all areas of our lives, influencing our thoughts, words, and actions. We could say that honor is not just *known*, it is also *shown*.

For us to show honor when it is due (whether toward God or man), we must first recognize that the occasion to show honor exists. Those called to ministry have occasion to bring honor every day to their own call, for being a minister in the Body of Christ is one of the highest privileges available on earth. It is regrettable that not all who occupy the ministry offices listed in Ephesians 4 and 1 Corinthians 12 recognize the greatness of their place. Likewise, many in the ministry of helps don't give their place of service the honor that it deserves. Notice in the Bible how Paul encouraged believers to recognize the importance of their place:

> *I THEREFORE, the prisoner for the Lord, appeal to and beg you to walk **(lead a life) worthy of the [divine] calling to which you have been called** [with behavior that is a credit to the summons to God's service.]*
> *Ephesians 4:1 (AMP)*

We all will stand before God one day to give an account of our actions, attitudes, and motives. How did we treat the place of service that God assigned to us? Did we just go through the motions? God's not looking for those who only focus on completing a set of tasks; He's looking for those with a right heart. He's looking for honor in ministry.

HOW TO LOSE EVERYTHING — THE STORY OF ELI

Thank God for those who have served well in ministry, leaving an example that others can follow. The Bible is filled with accounts of such ministry heroes. I'm glad however, that space was also given in the Word to show what happens when a minister doesn't walk worthy of his or her call. In the Bible, the poster-child for dishonor in ministry is a priest named Eli. The following passage is the Lord's rebuke to him:

> *Why then do you scorn my sacrifices and my offerings that I commanded for my dwelling, and **honor your sons above me** by fattening yourselves on the choicest parts of every offering of my people Israel?' Therefore the Lord, the God of Israel, declares: 'I promised that your house and the house of your father should go in and out before me forever,' but now the Lord declares: 'Far be it from me, **for those who honor me I will honor, and those who despise me shall be lightly esteemed.***
>
> *1 Samuel 2:29-30*

Eli and his sons didn't just have flesh problems, they had heart issues, despising what should have been honored. The word *despise* in the scriptures means *to fail to esteem*. To *esteem* means *to give the proper weight* to a person or thing. We despise when we don't assign something its proper weight or value, and this happens every day in the Kingdom of God by people who should know better. Eli and his sons treated the ministry with an air of lightness instead of with the heavy weight it deserved. It is interesting that in the original languages of scripture, one meaning of the word *honor* is *heavy* or *weighty*. We honor appropriately only when we give the things of God and the people of God their proper weight.

Those who are familiar with the story of Eli's family know that because they didn't properly esteem their places of ministry, they lost those places permanently. Could that same thing happen in our day? Without question. God has never changed, and although His mercy and patience are great, He will not allow His holy things to be treated with lightness. As one reads through 1 Samuel 2, it's easy to see some of the ways that dishonor manifested in Eli's ministry:

1. He and his sons failed to handle ministry money (offerings) correctly. God's money is *heavier* than ours and must not be treated casually.
2. They were poor stewards of the spiritual truths with which they were entrusted.

3. They used their positions of influence to manipulate and seduce others.

4. They made the house of God an unsafe place.

5. Eli respected family ties more than his responsibilities toward God.

All of the transgressions of Eli's house stemmed from a lack of honor toward God and the place of service to which He had called them. We must not repeat Eli's mistakes, but must instead understand that honor for God and for His ministry is something that must be maintained throughout the course of our lives.

Avoiding Familiarity

Is not this the carpenter's son? Is not his mother called Mary? And are not his brothers James and Joseph and Simon and Judas? And they took offense at him. But Jesus said to them, "A prophet is not without honor except in his hometown and in his own household." And he did not do many mighty works there, because of their unbelief.

Matthew 13:56-58

When honor is not in place, the inevitable result is *familiarity*. Familiarity occurs over time as one's view of a person or thing shifts from *special* to *common*. Less weight is given to that which was once weighty and important. It is not usually the case that the *actual value* of the person or item has changed but that *our view* of that person or item has changed.

One of the clearest examples of familiarity at work is in the marriage relationship. During courtship, the man treats the woman like the princess she truly is. Gifts flow freely and the car door is always opened for her right on time. She always takes time to look her best and gives him the attention he craves. Two months after the wedding day, all these efforts cease as the routines of life take over. Familiarity has set in. She no longer feels like the princess she once was, and he no longer feels like her hero. Because the special attentions have waned, frustrations mount and tensions increase. If this isn't quickly rectified, the marriage will unravel until it dies. Both parties must avoid familiarity by remembering their vows and honoring one another, each giving their spouse the proper weight and esteem. Everyone in a marriage relationship (or a work relationship, ministry, etc.) would do well to remember the words of Jesus:

> *Remember therefore from where you have fallen; repent, and* **do the works you did at first**. *If not, I will come to you and remove your lampstand from its place, unless you repent.*
>
> *Revelation 2:5*

What we fail to honor, we stand to lose. Just like many marriages have decayed until they have become unsalvageable, Eli's family forever lost everything that was truly valuable.

HONOR REQUIRES EFFORT

Maintaining honor is not difficult, but it is by no means automatic. Constant effort must be exercised to see and keep things in their right place. Honor's effort is not an option, but a necessity, for when honor is not in place, serious consequences can result. Many do not realize that a lack of honor is a violation of spiritual law, which not even God is able to set aside.

The apostle Paul taught and demonstrated the importance of bringing honor to the things of God. Throughout his ministry, he made the effort to maintain a humble attitude, expressing gratitude for his place of service.

I'm so grateful to Christ Jesus for making me adequate to do this work. He went out on a limb, you know, in trusting me with this ministry.

1 Timothy 1:12 (MSG)

True humility is displayed here through Paul. The letters he wrote to Timothy were written toward the end of his earthly life and ministry. In the many years since his conversion, Paul had accomplished much, yet he was still overwhelmed that God was willing to use him. Friends, let me tell you, it takes *effort* to maintain that kind of perspective. One must walk close to the Lord, keep the flesh crucified, and the mind renewed in order to see things as God sees them.

Notice that Paul didn't just keep honor in his heart; he gave expression to what was in his heart, voicing his gratitude to God for the tremendous place of ministry he was given. If we will bring a similar measure of honor to our God-ordained place, we will, like Paul, tap into a level of ministerial effectiveness that few have experienced.

CHAPTER 9

Honoring Your Gift

Now I am speaking to you Gentiles. Inasmuch then as I am an apostle to the Gentiles,
I magnify my ministry.
Romans 11:13

...I lay great stress on my ministry and magnify my office. (AMP)

...I make much of my ministry. (NIV)

...I do my ministry honor. (WST)

For the benefit of those who may be unfamiliar with the phrase *ministry offices*, it refers to divinely appointed places of service in the Body of Christ. The most recognized ministry offices are those we think of as full-time pulpit ministries:

the pastor, evangelist, teacher, prophet, and apostle. Each office shares elements in common with the others, yet each has its own distinct characteristics and anointing. There are, of course, other offices and ministries mentioned in the Word of God that support the preaching offices. These supportive ministries are worthy of no less honor than the others.

The potential exists today for these offices to bring forth the same depth of power that they did in Jesus' ministry. However, whether or not they operate at their full potential depends largely on the level of spiritual development of the minister. Just like an engine can have a governor on it, capping its performance below potential, the full potential of the ministry offices are capped by the faith, spirituality, and lifestyle of the minister. Over time, the minister must grow and develop into the full potential of his or her ministry. One of the components that will allow that growth to occur is honor. The minister must assign his or her ministry its proper weight and value, recognizing the greatness of their place (even if it looks small and somewhat insignificant in its present form.)

Your place of service in the Body of Christ is an amazing thing. See it that way, and you will guard it, care for it, and value it, even speaking words of faith about it. As you do these things, you will unlock the potential of your place, rising up and fulfilling all God has called you to do.

AN ANOINTING-FRIENDLY LIFESTYLE

We recognize that the element that makes our place of ministry great is God's precious anointing. Every part of our lives must cater to that anointing if it is to develop into its fullness. All the qualifications for ministry listed in the New Testament must be embraced. For example, the minister cannot fail to be honorable with his physical body and expect to fulfill his ministry to Christ's Body.

There are other good books that have been written about these qualifications for ministry, so I'll only give the subject minimal coverage here.

> *Do not be unequally yoked with unbelievers. For what partnership has righteousness with lawlessness? Or what fellowship has light with darkness? What accord has Christ with Belial? Or what portion does a believer share with an unbeliever? What agreement has the temple of God with idols? For we are the temple of the living God; as God said, "I will make my dwelling among them and walk among them, and I will be their God, and they shall be my people. Therefore go out from their midst, and **be separate from them**, says the Lord, and **touch no unclean thing**; then I will welcome you, and I will be a father to you, and you shall be sons and daughters to me, says the Lord Almighty."*
>
> *2 Corinthians 6:16-18*

An individual can be called by God to a place of ministry, but that call alone does not guarantee success. Attention must first be given to another call – one that precedes any great ministry – the call to live a life separated to God.

Notice in the passage we just read that the believer is blessed with an amazing privilege: the experience of true union in the family of God. We can be close with The Creator. This degree of oneness is available to all of God's children, but it is only experienced by those who practice the passage in its entirety. Intimacy with the Father requires more than just being *in Christ*; it also requires separation from that which is unclean.

What is unclean? Most of what is in the world. Most of what is on television. Most movies. Most music. Even much of what is labeled *Christian* entertainment is full of doubt and unbelief. Honoring our place of ministry means that we maintain a degree of separation from the filth that is in the world. Many ministers claim to know these truths, even teaching them to others, yet they watch late-night TV every Saturday before preaching on Sunday morning. That's not enough separation if we are to be effective.

What we take in through our senses affects our spiritual life and our ministerial effectiveness. There is such a thing as wholesome entertainment. Some of that can be healthy, but *too much* will compromise our anointing. The minister that doesn't see the need to set boundaries, limiting what they take in from the world, doesn't yet know the anointing like he or she should. It has been my experience that, if we want greater measures of anointing, greater separation from the world is required.

I know this may sound extreme to some, but do we want God's anointing and power or not? Christians, even preachers, watch comedies that are filthy, and sit there, laughing out-of-control. The believer who is sensitive to the fact that God is personally present within them should be horrified at what they see and hear, instead of being entertained. There is such a thing as clean comedy. Find those kinds of movies and watch them once in a while if you want.

Some believers and ministers are always recommending romance movies to their friends. I like those movies when they are clean, but it seems like few are. A Christian (especially a minister) has no business looking at naked bodies other than that of their spouse. Look away, or step out of the room if necessary. If it is just plain indecent or dirty, turn it off. Don't let the fact that you paid for the movie be an excuse to expose your spirit to something that will bring you down to a lower place. Honor your place by honoring the indwelling Christ, and see how He honors you with more of His presence.

Seeing Ourselves As God Sees Us

*From now on, therefore, **we regard no one according to the flesh**. Even though we once regarded Christ according to the flesh, we regard him thus no longer.*

2 Corinthians 5:16

We all know it would be a mistake to see Jesus as only a carpenter, but it is just as wrong to see ourselves only according to our natural stations in life. Every believer has a place in Christ, and a place of service, or ministry, in the Body. Ministers must have the humility to realize that they can accomplish nothing on their own, but also have the faith to see themselves functioning with all the equipment that God has given them. I must learn to see myself as God sees me: standing in my ministry office, fully developed. Only then will I rise up and fulfill my call in its entirety.

As we seek to make the most of our office, we must be cautious not to compare ourselves with other ministers or ministries. We thank God for those that inspire us, but we look only to Jesus when measuring our ministry. He is our standard, no one else. We also must guard against pride, being careful not to think of ourselves more highly than we ought (Romans 12:3). Remember, we are respecting our *office*, not promoting ourselves.

Many today who are called to places of ministry fail to properly honor their God-ordained place. They walk by sight and in the flesh, measuring their gifts only by natural indicators such as the present size of their ministry. Such thinking will cause that ministry to remain at a low level of effectiveness. By faith, see a picture of your ministry by looking at the ministry of Jesus, and then concentrate on progressing in your anointing. While you are showing honor for your office by honing your skills, God will often respond by adding new dimensions of ministry to you. Don't be the one-talent kind of servant, but be the faithful one that God can bless.

Bringing full honor to your place of ministry will require some sacrifice where your time is concerned. Waiting on God, sometimes for extended seasons, will be necessary in order to ensure you are fulfilling *His* plan, not your own. It may take more commitment and effort than you originally thought, but your place is worth the price. Honor your office; see it as big as it is. Do your ministry honor by giving it all the weight it deserves.

CHAPTER 10

Honoring The Gifts In Others

But as it is, God arranged the members in the body, each one of them, as he chose. If all were a single member, where would the body be? As it is, there are many parts, yet one body.

And on those parts of the body that we think less honorable we bestow the greater honor.
1 Corinthians 12:18-20,22

Believers (ministers included) must learn to recognize the gifts of others in the Body, for now more than ever, the one-man-show mentality in the Body of Christ will not work. In grade school, an *I* on an assignment means *incomplete*. That's also true in the Church and in ministry. Anytime it's just *I*, realize that something is missing from the equation: other people. There are no solo acts in the Kingdom of God, so it is essential that we correctly relate to others who have also answered the call to serve.

VIEWING OTHER MINISTERS HONORABLY

Ministers must not fall into the trap of seeing their own ministry as the standard by which they compare other ministries. That is nothing more than pride and carnality, yet it happens all the time. Just as we are advised in the scriptures not to compare ourselves to others (2 Corinthians 10:12), we should certainly not make the greater mistake of *comparing others to ourselves* (thinking *If you're not just like me, you're missing it*). It is right to be the kind of minister that is an example to others, but by no means are any one of us the standard to which all others should aspire. We must understand that wrong thinking in these areas leads us to see others in a less important light, and causes us to miss the benefits that we might otherwise receive from their gifts.

If you are a minister, there are other ministers in the Body who no doubt stand in a higher place of anointing than you, those who are somewhat equal to you, and those who are less developed than you. Which ones can God use to speak into *your* life? I understand that, as a usual thing, we are to look to those above us for our instruction, but honor has taught me to be open to receive from anyone that God would choose to use. To say that we cannot receive from someone who is younger or supposedly less anointed than we are would be like saying we don't need the less prominent parts of our physical body. I love the following verse in which some less prominent members of the body of Christ were used to minister to one of the most prominent members:

> *I rejoice at the coming of Stephanas and Fortunatus and Achaicus, because they have made up for your absence, for **they refreshed my spirit** as well as yours. Give recognition to such people.*
>
> 1 Corinthians 16:17-18

Everyone knows Paul. Almost no one knows Stephanas, Fortunatus, and Achaicus, yet these three in some way ministered spiritual refreshment to Paul. I imagine that all three together were not his spiritual equal, yet he still received something precious from them. It is a show of disrespect for the anointing of God when we disregard the ministry of another. Do not discount the place of those you deem less developed than yourself or you may miss out on refreshment and other spiritual benefits. Their ministry gift is still from God and is worthy of honor.

OUT OF THE BOX

*There is no lack of room for you in [our hearts], but you lack room in your own affections [for us]. By way of return then, do this for me—I speak as to children—**open wide your hearts** also [to us].*

2 Corinthians 6:12-13 (AMP)

We must make room in our own hearts for others to develop in ministry. If you heard someone preach who was just starting out, it would be easy to form an opinion of them, capping them in your heart and mind at that beginning level. We must avoid that error, for it limits how God can use them in our lives later on. God is in the business of growing ministers and ministries. For example, there are some ministry circles in which I am known exclusively as a saxophone player. Over the years, God has developed other gifts in me, such as my preaching ministry, yet many still see me only as a saxophonist. Others, who knew me as a pastor, continue to see me only in that capacity, though I haven't served in that office for some time now. As ministers progress and transition through the stages of their ministry, those who would receive from them must also change, being willing to see them differently.

People tend to put others in a box, so to speak, based on their initial exposure to their ministry. This is another example of familiarity at work. Let's instead be looking for our fellow ministers to develop over time into higher anointings and offices. The people in Jesus' hometown never made the heart-adjustment from carpenter to prophet, and therefore could not receive from His ministry. Think of what they missed by not making room in their hearts for His anointing. These heart issues are also honor issues. How important it is that we see others through the eyes of honor.

When ministers make mistakes, we must not write them off in our minds as permanently disqualified. Paul was burned in ministry by one of his helpers, a young minister named Mark. Mark's unfaithfulness no doubt created added pressure for Paul at the time, and Paul was right in not using Mark for a season. However, honor for the gift of God in Mark helped Paul to avoid keeping Mark in the box of unfaithfulness. How precious it is to see Paul later making a demand on the gift of God in Mark:

> *Luke alone is with me. Get Mark and bring him with you, for **he is very useful to me for ministry**.*
> *2 Timothy 4:11*

Could it have been this vote of confidence and show of honor by Paul that helped Mark move on from his past mistakes and embrace the awesome assignment of writing the gospel that bears his name? Do not put others in a box based on what you see or hear in the natural. Be like God. He continues to believe in people, and His gifts and callings are irrevocable (Romans 11:29).

TALKING ABOUT OTHERS IN MINISTRY

DO NOT judge and criticize and condemn others, so that you may not be judged and criticized and condemned yourselves. For just as you judge and criticize and condemn others, you will be judged and criticized and condemned, and in accordance with the measure you [use to] deal out to others, it will be dealt out again to you.

Matthew 7:1-2 (AMP)

Preachers must discuss different ministry issues among themselves, and in doing so sometimes refer to the practices of other ministers, but there are lines that must not be crossed. Whether we agree with certain ministers, we must respect the fact that God chose to call them to their place. Even when ministers fail to honor their own place, we must honor it.

If any person ever had good reason to verbally trash the place of another, it was David as he dealt with King Saul. Saul had truly disqualified himself from his place of service, but David, the God-appointed heir to that place, refused to use Saul's blunders to his own advantage. David took the high road when much lesser men would have taken matters into their own hands. As Saul allowed the devil to wreak havoc in the kingdom, David sat by and watched the whole uncomfortable drama unfold. Only after Saul perished on his own and the people recognized David's call and anointing did he step into the place that Saul had once occupied. What an example of honor!

Much of what goes on after church services at the dinner table is gossip, and such judgment does not flow from the Spirit of God. When people talk about their pastor, or another minister, their dishonor removes them from the anointing that would have blessed their life. Even if a minister has missed it, we do not want to use our mouths to hasten their downfall. We want them to make the necessary corrections and be restored to their place if possible. My place is never increased or enhanced by the failures of others. I look best when others in ministry also look good. We must learn that ministry is simply not a competition or a race run *against* others.

CHAPTER 11

Honoring Those Over You

Just as God connects every believer to a pastor and local church, He places every minister in a spiritual family with proper oversight. In my years of ministry, I have yet to see *one* minister who took the island-to-themselves approach and was successful. In many cases, great failure occurred in their life. In every case, full potential was not achieved. The Word of God is clear that we are to find, and stay in, our place in His family.

> *God sets the solitary in families; He brings out those who are bound into prosperity; But the rebellious dwell in a dry land.*
>
> Psalm 68:6 (NKJV)

*And being let go, they went to **their own company**, and reported all that the chief priests and elders had said unto them.*

Acts 4:23 (KJV)

Obey your leaders and submit to them, for they are keeping watch over your souls, as those who will have to give an account. Let them do this with joy and not with groaning, for that would be of no advantage to you.

Hebrews 13:17

We must bring honor to those whom God has placed over us in ministry. There are a few primary ways this is accomplished. The first level of honor we must bring toward our leaders is an inward recognition of their place. Only when we see them correctly in our own heart will we give proper weight to their place in our lives.

Do not seek to be treated as a friend or an equal by those over you. My spiritual elders have allowed me to enjoy close fellowship with them at times, but I understand that it is my job to maintain an awareness of their place, avoiding familiarity. I do not compare my ministry skills with theirs because that is irrelevant. They are not my elders because they beat me in a preaching competition, have a bigger ministry than I, or have more books in print. God has ordained their place in my life.

TITLES IN THE BODY OF CHRIST

We also bring honor to those who are over us by *referring* to them with honor. We understand that many have gotten into error by seeking special titles and using them to feed their egos, but the fact that some have gone to the extreme does not do away with the truth in the middle of the road. When people have a place above us, whether spiritually, on the job, or in a family, they should be referred to by their proper title. It helps us remember our place, and it helps them know that we recognize their place.

I don't call a police officer by his or her first name. Nor would I do the same with a judge, schoolteacher, or congressman. Why then, have we decided that ministers are no longer worthy of the title that designates their office? I call my pastor "Pastor" because that's what God put him in my life to be. Calling him by his first name places him on a natural level, a level equal with myself. That is the last thing I want. My pastor's place as a *person* benefits me far less than his place as a minister. I refer to him by his ministry title because I want a manifestation of that office in my life. If we see people only in the natural, referring to them as we would natural friends, we will have difficulty receiving from the anointing on their life. We must do what it takes to recognize the anointing so we can better receive from the anointing.

When I am around a fellow minister, whether in a service or at a casual or fellowship event, I refer to them using their ministry title. I am not just trying to be formal; I refuse to see them only according to their humanity. I discipline myself to see them with their anointing. When I speak to them, I want them to know that their place of service is honored, even if they have only occupied it for a short while.

Many might find this extreme, but I even like to refer to fellow believers as "brother" or "sister so-and-so" instead of only using their natural names. "Brother John" lets John know that I see him *in Christ*, not just as a natural man. It helps me avoid familiarity and helps to create a culture of honor, which is desperately needed. Commonality and casualness are at epidemic levels and must be countered with honor.

Church culture today would do away with all titles, so no one feels as though they must submit to anyone else. Following that culture removes the awareness of the anointing from ministry settings. These practices seem harmless but they are actually devilish! Let's stay out of the ditch of empty formality, but let's also stay out of the ditch of commonality.

Financial and Material Honor

*One day Elisha went on to Shunem, where a rich and influential woman lived, who insisted on his eating a meal. Afterward, whenever he passed by, he stopped there for a meal. And she said to her husband, Behold now, **I perceive that this is a holy man of God** who passes by continually. Let us make a small chamber on the [housetop] and put there for him a bed, a table, a chair, and a lamp. Then whenever he comes to us, he can go [up the outside stairs and rest] here.*

2 Kings 4:8-10 (AMP)

We don't know if this woman had previously received from Elisha's ministry, but we do know that she was able to recognize the greatness that was within him. More than just honoring him in her heart or with an appropriate title, this woman knew that honor is only complete when it acts honorably. Although her efforts were directed at meeting a physical need in Elisha's life, the honor behind her actions also initiated a spiritual transaction, connecting her to his anointing. She later received a tremendous harvest as a result of her show of honor.

This woman understood that spiritual and natural things often work together, the actions of each realm affecting the other. She also understood that a minister's spiritual effectiveness can be enhanced by his natural comfort. The Church today must receive this revelation, taking care of those in ministry by showing them financial and material honor.

The world only gives when there is an apparent pressing need. Although there are times when it is appropriate to give to help meet a need, the Church should be accomplished at all other forms of giving as well: Spirit-led giving, Word-based giving, and something we could call *honor-based giving*. With honor-based giving, the weight and value of the person's anointing and place creates the need, not their financial condition. When giving out of honor, we don't even need to know whether a natural need is present. The debt of honor is due regardless. The absence of a physical need does not make the show of honor unnecessary.

The tithes and offerings we bring to our local church are a show of honor toward God (see Proverbs 3:9.) His honor always comes first. We should not stop there however. It is also appropriate to honor our ministry leaders personally, regularly sowing into their lives. These gifts do not buy us any natural influence in their ministry, but since honor is a spiritual flow from the heart, financial honor can enhance our *spiritual connection* with the ministry or minister. Our expressions of honor, love, and generosity toward them have a boomerang effect in the spirit-realm, causing great things to come back toward us. We must always remain open-hearted to give, so that we will have the capacity of heart to receive when the time comes (we will see an example of this shortly in the Shunamite woman's life.)

Words cannot express the importance of the spiritual connection created by honor. Again, we are not suggesting that we can buy influence with God, or that we are to try to buy our way into favor with the ministers God has placed in our life. This is something genuine and from the heart, not something proceeding from false motives or as a result of manipulation. While we are aware of the delicate balance in this area, we must not neglect to teach the value of these expressions of honor for fear that some may misunderstand or misapply the truth. I can certainly testify that the ministries and ministers I have sown into have brought a supply into my life that has far exceeded the value of my monetary gifts.

Think about the gift the Shunamite woman bestowed upon Elisha. Not many believers today would build an addition on to their house (or a separate guest house) just to refresh a minister. Most would say that even the thought of such a gift would be inappropriate and excessive. In many cases however, honor justifies bestowing gifts that the un-renewed mind would deem extravagant. Our culture has taught us to look critically at the minister's blessings (as though the minister needs help monitoring his possessions), but we must reject the wrong thinking of our culture. Let's instead be concerned with the spiritual connections and benefits that come as we show honor to the people of God.

Several years ago, my wife and I discovered a waterfront property for sale on a lake, not too far from our home. The view was gorgeous. Although we had desired such a property for our own enjoyment, I was equally excited at the prospect of using this property to bless and refresh other ministers. We were able to do that on several occasions. There were a few times when we were privileged to house missionaries there for weeks at a time, and they were so blessed to have a place to live, sit, enjoy the view, rest, and hear from Heaven without any expense on their part. Truthfully, it took all the money and faith we had to acquire and maintain that property, but if we went through all of it just to bring refreshment to one of the great men and women of God who enjoyed it over the years, it was worth it.

In the case of the Shunemite woman, the connection she established with Elisha's ministry paid rich dividends. A son was born to her supernaturally, and when that son fell sick and died, he was raised up by Elisha's anointing. The benefits that she received as a result of her show of honor to the prophet far surpassed the sacrifice that she and her husband had made. Like this woman, believers in the Church today should practice the Word and be open to the leading of the Spirit, actively believing for the provision necessary to minister great blessing to those who are specially anointed and used of God.

Whether in full-time ministry, or as a volunteer in ministry, let us bring full honor to the work of God. As we do, our ministries will become recipients of honor, both in heaven and on earth.

[We have discussed honor in ministry in a way that can apply to all believers, however there are many other areas of honor in ministry that are unique to those in full-time preaching ministries. A detailed discussion of some of these areas has been included toward the back of this book, in The Appendix.]

Honor

in

Life

CHAPTER 12

Honor Means Doing What's Right

Although I wasn't raised in a Christian home, I was raised having been religiously educated. Born-again people are understandably repulsed by most of what religion (any non-life-producing system of worship) includes, but one thing it does well is to instill a sense of right and wrong in people.

Over the years I have observed many religious people living alongside those who were supposedly true Christians. Sadly, the unsaved religious person often outshines the believer when it comes to good old-fashioned decency. I lived for many years in a predominantly Catholic region and found many of the religiously-educated Catholic young men to be some of the most polite, respectful, and right-living people I have ever met. I was raised Jewish and have been around many Jews who had these same qualities, living better lives than many who call themselves Spirit-filled believers.

I had long wondered why this was so, and eventually realized that there are portions of scripture to which religious people gravitate. Because the Old Testament, and even the gospels, were from a time before people could be born-again, parts of it can be easily understood by people who are not born-again. These parts of scripture deal more with the behavior of man than with the things of the Spirit – passages like the Ten Commandments and The Beatitudes. These passages show us what it means to live right and do right. Born-again believers are correct to dwell in the pages of the New Testament letters, but we must not neglect these other parts of the Word and the lessons contained therein.

> *Here is a simple, rule-of-thumb guide for behavior: Ask yourself what you want people to do for you, then grab the initiative and do it for them. Add up God's Law and Prophets and this is what you get.*
>
> *Matthew 7:12 (MSG)*

Christians have the advantage of the indwelling Spirit, who unveils the Living Word and gives real-time feedback and input for right-living. We ought to be the ones leading the way in decency, morality, love, and honor. We ought to do right and live right.

AN EARLY LESSON IN HONOR

Although we were raised with good values, my brother and I still managed to find our way into plenty of trouble as we were growing up. One day however, the things we were taught at home and in Religious School (that's what our Jewish Temple called our Sunday morning training) were put to the test. Thankfully, what was in us rose to the top.

We were out (either walking or riding our bikes) near one of the city parks, several blocks from home, when our wildest dreams came true. There, right in front of us in the grass with no one else around, was a field full of money, nothing smaller than twenty dollar bills. (My Mom probably thought we were both physically handicapped, because when we were required to pick up the mess in our bedrooms, we seemed unable to comply. All of our limbs were suddenly loosed however when we saw that money.) We got every bit of it in a matter of seconds, and then found a wallet nearby. Normally, finding a wallet would have been exciting, but it was rather unpleasant to find after raking in all the cash, because it identified the owner of the money. My first thought was to bury it, but we knew better.

I'm not sure that we had any idea what to do with hundreds of dollars in cash, but just having it was great. There was no way we weren't going to let our parents know about it though. We secured all the money and high-tailed it home to turn it in to Mom and Dad. I think I remember my Mom talking to us about how the right thing to do was to call the owner and try and return it. We knew that was right, but you can understand the mixed feelings we had about giving up our newfound wealth.

I'll never forget the scene that evening when a man came to our house and rang our doorbell. My brother and I stood there listening as the man told us that his wife was in the hospital delivering their first child. The cash we had found was all he had to his name, and it was just enough to pay the hospital bill. He was so excited about his baby being born that, after going to the bank, he mindlessly set his wallet on the dash of his car as he drove back to the hospital. When he turned a corner, the wallet flew out the window just moments before the Siegel boys came by. This man was so relieved to be able to pay that hospital bill. In fact, he pulled out a few bills and gave them to my Mom so she could take our family out to dinner. That wasn't our biggest reward, however. The real reward was a recognition inside of us that we had done something honorable. We learned that honor means doing what is right.

*Who may worship in your sanctuary, Lord? Who may enter your presence on your holy hill? Those who lead blameless lives and **do what is right**, speaking the truth from sincere hearts. Those who refuse to gossip or harm their neighbors or speak evil of their friends. Those who despise flagrant sinners, and honor the faithful followers of the Lord, and **keep their promises even when it hurts**. Those who lend money without charging interest, and who cannot be bribed to lie about the innocent. Such people will stand firm forever.*

Psalm 15 (NLT)

[Explanation: Way back in the 1970's and 1980's, dashboards in cars were not deep and contoured as they are now. They were more like a shelf where people would store things like cigarettes, or stuffed animals, and if you really weren't thinking straight, a wallet.]

[Explanation #2 (for our kids): Not every car had air conditioning back then, so people would drive with the windows down to get fresh air. They actually would have to physically crank a handle to lower or raise the window. That's why some still use the phrase "rolling the window down".]

CHAPTER 13

Integrity Keeps Us Safe

People of honor are people of principle, conviction, and backbone; people who can be counted on to do the right thing. Have you ever met someone like that? Someone with such integrity that you didn't dare ask them to fudge the numbers? Such people are awesome to behold, for they are a rare breed in a world that has far too many cheats and liars. Every Christian should be a person of honor and integrity.

I like the word *integrity*. I like how it's used to describe buildings. You've heard the phrase *structural integrity*. That means no matter how much you poke around, you won't find weakness.

I once sold a house with wood siding. The buyers sent a home inspector out to check out the house, and I was startled when he pulled out what looked like an ice pick and started poking at the siding. On the side of the house that didn't get much sun, his ice pick went right into one of the boards (which of course, I had to replace). That wood had lost its integrity; it was rotten or decayed. When we pulled that board off the house, we didn't save it for another project, because you can't build anything with rotten wood. How many believers have areas of their lives with compromised integrity? Sure, they're still a precious part of the Body of Christ, but parts of their lives have suffered decay and are rotting. God can't build anything with their lives.

We don't want any rotten, soft spots in our lives, our churches, our communities, or our nation. When wood is rotten, it is often filled with bugs. Wood with integrity on the other hand is resistant to most bugs. Honor and integrity in one's life will cause that life to be resistant to the enemy, and that person will be kept safe. The compromised life, on the other hand, is one that is easily penetrated by the enemy.

Compromise in people's lives spills over to affect our communities and nation. I believe that much of the natural disaster that plagues our nation could be avoided if sin wasn't so prevalent. Sin will weaken a people, making them vulnerable to the enemy.

> *God-devotion makes a country strong; God-avoidance leaves people weak.*
>
> *Proverbs 14:34 (MSG)*

Certain regions in our country (for instance, portions of the coastal areas) seem to be gathering places for immorality and godlessness. I believe the high concentration of sin compromises the integrity of those regions, and those areas become more susceptible to disaster as a result. We can ill-afford any more soft-spots in our country where our enemies, human or demonic, can penetrate our defenses. Both personally and nationally, we must be people of honor and strong integrity, doing right and living right.

CHAPTER 14

Lying Our Way Through Life

God can't stomach liars; He loves the company of
those who keep their word.
Proverbs 12:22 (MSG)

Lying is a way of life for most of the world. People think nothing of it, and it's how a good portion of the daily business of our country is conducted. It's still wrong and, according to the verse above, it nauseates the Lord. It ought to make us sick, too.

Many Christians lie as much as unsaved people lie. Lying will always be prevalent where there is no culture of honor. However, the honorable man is a man of his word. Those we might call old-timers used to have a saying that we would be smart to resurrect: *If your word is no good, you're no good.*

Why is lying such a big deal? The bigger question is why the Body of Christ thinks it's *not* a big deal. Notice this verse from the gospel of John:

> *For you are the children of your father the devil, and you love to do the evil things he does. He was a murderer from the beginning. He has always hated the truth, because there is no truth in him.* **When he lies, it is consistent with his character; for he is a liar and the father of lies.**
>
> *John 8:44 (NLT)*

A Christian who tells a lie is advertising to everyone, saved and unsaved, that he has aligned himself with the kingdom of darkness, and has decided to imitate the character and nature of the devil, instead of imitating God. Lying is one of the most dishonorable acts there is.

How many Christians would be willing to attend a satanic ritual where everyone bows in worship and pledges allegiance to the dark side? Almost no believer would participate in such an event, but so few realize that they are doing something very similar when they lie. The next time you are presented with an opportunity to speak falsely, perhaps it would be a good idea to picture yourself attending the satanist church! That mental picture may help you catch yourself before you misspeak. Another great deterrent for lying is to remember the story of Ananias and Sapphira (you can read about them in Acts chapter 5.) They lied themselves to death.

From Adam to the Antichrist, the pages of scripture offer accounts of people that lied, each case showing us that it is never the right route. Many are in the habit of lying, but don't realize how it affects their lives. Here are a few of the unwanted effects of lying:

1. Inability to distinguish truth from deception.
2. Inability to receive from God's Word. (If your word is no good, you will not be able to trust God's Word.)
3. Inability to successfully operate in faith. In order for faith to work, you must believe that *your* words are coming to pass. When one speaks falsely, the inner-man is trained not to believe the words spoken. Lying undermines the whole process of faith.
4. Loss of credibility. The one who lies is doubly deceived. First, they think that their lie will get them a positive result. Second, they think the one to whom they told the lie won't know. Friends, Christians are indwelt by the Spirit of Truth who bears witness to the truth. If a lie is told, the Spirit flags it right away. You will be caught.
5. Loss of fellowship with God.
6. Feelings of condemnation and guilt.
7. Violation of conscience.

8. The knowledge that you were dishonorable.

That last point may not seem as weighty as the others but it should be. Honor should be so important to the believer that the loss of it would be devastating. I'd rather lose my house, car, and other possessions than to lose my honor. I could get another house more quickly than I could restore honor, for honor is the sum total of a person's character built up over the course of an entire life. If lost, it is not quickly regained.

NO MORE LIES

And GOD said, 'How can we seduce Ahab into attacking Ramoth Gilead?' Some said this, and some said that. Then a bold angel stepped out, stood before GOD, and said, 'I'll seduce him.' 'And how will you do it?' said GOD. **'Easy,' said the angel, 'I'll get all the prophets to lie.'**

1 Kings 22:20-22 (MSG)

It shouldn't be easy to get a minister to tell a lie. Ministers must be people of their word, leading the way in truth. I bring this up, not to talk about others, but to tell about a lie I told after having been in full-time ministry for well over twenty years!

I wish I hadn't lied, but I did it, and I decided well in advance to do it. The state in which I live has some auto registration fees that are downright ungodly. When I moved to my state, I eventually got around to registering our automobiles. It actually took longer than I had planned because I had to retitle one of the cars. When I registered that vehicle, the agent at the Motor Vehicles Office asked when I brought it into the state. I truthfully answered, telling them the exact date I moved. *Then* they told me I had waited too long to register it and would be fined an extra $50 per overdue month. I was livid; I wrote the check and left. I don't like paying more than I have to for anything.

A few months later I realized that I had never registered one of our motorcycles. It was winter, and the bike had been covered up in the garage with my old, but still valid, out-of-state tag on it. I decided that the DMV was not going to trick me again into a several-hundred-dollar donation. I planned out my answer to the "When did you bring the vehicle in-state" question ahead of time and went to get it registered. I justified my lie by telling myself that, since I still owned property in my previous state, I had every right to pretend that the vehicle had been there the whole time. When the lady at the DMV looked at me and asked when I brought the vehicle in, I looked her square in the eye and told her a flat-out lie. I lied like a real pro that day. Everything went perfectly, except I walked out of that place feeling like I might die of a heart attack. I had grieved God in a major way. I guess I turned His stomach.

I got into the car feeling horribly. I immediately repented to my wife, who had been present. Why? Because she knows me as a man of God and a man of my word, and I have no right to expect her to have to sit and listen to filth coming out of my mouth. No, I didn't curse, I lied, which is far more filthy, and totally dishonorable. My mouth belongs to God, not the devil.

My wife forgave me, but God still wanted to talk to me. He was actually most kind about it. He spoke to my heart and said, "Son, you know you could have just believed me for the extra money to pay the fine, and it would have come in." Right. I actually had never thought about that. I'm a faith preacher, and using my faith never even occurred to me. What is $250 to God? Absolutely nothing. He can get that to me any day without breaking a sweat. What is the cost of a lie? Way more than $250. Thank God for His mercy. No more lying.

LIED TO FOR A LIVING

I am more familiar with lying than I wish to be. Lying is not my habit, but it has nonetheless been a big part of my life. I have been a professional musician for about 30 years. For several years, I owned an apartment complex. I have been in full-time ministry for over two decades. Between the three occupations, I have been lied to constantly. I hate it, just like God hates it.

The musicians have been the least problematic, as over the years I have graduated to the kind of work that is very enjoyable and above-board. The apartment tenants were mostly people who lived a low level of existence anyway. They were lost and were just being true to who they were. It's the Christians I could never figure out. How could someone who claimed to be born-again still live like they were a child of the devil?

As a pastor, I had wonderful church members, but when factoring in visitors, I estimate I was lied to almost every week. I usually knew it the moment it happened. People would visit the church and tell me, "We loved it. We'll be back next week." I finally learned that what they really meant was, "You will never, ever see us again." Church members would sign up to help with a ministry project and not show up. They lied to their pastor. If you said you'd be there and just didn't show up, you lied. If you said you'd be somewhere at a certain time, and showed up an hour late without communicating to anyone, you lied. That's a big deal. *Any* lie is a big deal.

People who pledge money for a ministry project, and then don't give it, are liars. No one forced them to give their pledge, but they did. Once your word has been given, fulfilling that word should be your main pursuit. Our word must be a bigger deal to us than the money.

When someone lies to me, they just told me, "I don't honor or respect you or the anointing on your life. I don't fear God.

I don't value your place in my life. You're nothing to me." I'd rather you spit in my face or punch me than lie to me.

Lies bring a person into bondage. Truth, on the other hand, sets a person free. People of honor are people who are completely committed to the truth.

CHAPTER 15

Honor And Honesty

Recompense to no man evil for evil. Provide things
honest in the sight of all men.
Romans 12:17 (KJV)

The spelling of the word *honest* reveals how close in meaning it is to the word *honor*. They are really one and the same. The honest individual brings an honor-building credibility and transparency to his or her life. Others are not so honest; it is difficult to refer to them as people of honor. It is possible for a person to technically not lie, but still mislead and deceive. That is dishonest, and can diminish our reputation in the sight of others.

I am thankful for those who have been good examples to me in this area of honesty. One of the things I most appreciated about Rev. Kenneth E. Hagin was the what-you-see-is-what-you-get sense of reality that marked his ministry and life. He laid the truth out honestly and avoided all the backpedaling, shucking & jiving, and lying that others have to do to try and save face.

A good test of how honest you are is to see how simply you can respond when questioned by others. Deceivers, who don't want to get caught in outright lies, must master the art of intricate answers:

"Where were you last night?"

"Well, let me tell you what happened. It's complicated . . . ."

> *Let your Yes be simply Yes, and your No be simply No;*
> *anything more than that comes from the evil one.*
>
> *Matthew 5:37 (AMP)*

Do you remember how Satan tried to complicate things with Eve in the garden? He works the same way today. If you frequently require legal counsel just to respond to situations at work or home, perhaps there needs to be a big shift towards honesty. That is not to say that we must always disclose every detail of our lives to everyone we know. If we learn to listen to our conscience, and keep it clear, it will safely guide us and we will know what's right to tell, and what's right to keep private.

Never violate your conscience (the voice of your spirit). Develop the habit of instantly obeying your inner man instead of allowing your mind to complicate and cloud the situation. Natural circumstances want your full attention and consideration, and it can be very tempting to take in wrong thoughts that would bring confusion. Become strong enough in spirit to hold yourself in the realm of peace, where there is clarity of conscience, honesty, and honor.

Keep praying for us, for we are convinced that we have a good (clear) conscience, that we want to walk uprightly and live a noble life, **acting honorably and in complete honesty in all things.**

Hebrews 13:18 (AMP)

HONESTY AT HOME

Honesty is a big issue within the marriage relationship. Husbands and wives should have no secrets between them. Many marriages are filled with lies, secrets, and deception. That's too much trouble for me. I have too much to keep track of without having to remember which version of a story I told my wife. If there is no honesty, there can be no trust. If there's no trust, how can there be a real marriage? If you have been keeping secrets from your spouse, you must come clean. It may cause trouble in the short-term, but it will be far better in the long-term.

When we had new television service installed in our home, the installer told us something that we could hardly believe. He said, "You would be shocked at how many homes I go to for installation, where the husband leaves to go to the shed, basement, or garage, reappearing moments later with a brand new giant-screen television that his wife didn't know was purchased." This installer said that several times a month, he has to sit and listen to a blow-out argument between a husband and wife before he knows whether it's okay for him to hook up the new TV. It's amazing to me how many adults have the maturity of a five-year-old. How could anyone expect their marriage to thrive under such conditions?

The only time it is acceptable to deceive or mislead anyone (spouse included) is during the days just before Christmas, anniversaries, and birthdays. When they ask, "What's in that box?" it's okay to respond, "Nothing that concerns you" (as long as it's really something nice for them . . . .)

We must grow to the place where our word is one-hundred percent reliable. If I say it, I will do it, whether it is convenient or not. Although I'm sure I could grow even more, I know I have developed over the years in this area. If I promise to be somewhere, I'm there at the time I said I would be there. If there is an issue beyond my control, such as a traffic situation, I call and let the other party know. If I say I'm giving money to someone, they should consider it in the bank. It will be there. I make sure that my word is always good, because I need my words working for me daily as I use my faith.

CHAPTER 16

Honor And Faithfulness

---

*Ahimelech answered the king, "There's not an official in
your administration as true to you* (faithful) *as David,
your own son-in-law and captain of your bodyguard.
None more honorable either."*
1 Samuel 22:14 (MSG)

There is a connection between faithfulness, loyalty, and
honor that must not be overlooked. Those in the world
(and many in the Church) pay little attention to these qualities; to many, they're just old-fashioned words without much
practical meaning. The child of God who is pursuing the life of
honor understands that these words represent qualities that
are as close as one can get to the nature of God.

God's faithfulness is unbroken. He will stay with you when
everyone else leaves. You can always count on Him because He

has never failed anyone, *ever*. It's not in His nature to selfishly turn His back on His family; He wouldn't know how to do it if He wanted to. That kind of faithfulness is what makes God so honorable. It's also what must be found in us if we are to be people of honor.

David is exalted in the scriptures as a person who was faithful and honorable. He wasn't perfect in the flesh, but God saw his faithfulness and loyalty and counted his heart as being perfect (see 1 Kings 11:4.) David proved himself faithful as a shepherd with his sheep and as a servant to King Saul. He left Saul only as a last resort, and left for the sake of everyone's peace, not to advance his own career or future. Faithfulness ran so deep in David that, even after enduring Saul's demonic fits of rage, it was difficult for him to jump ship and leave. We need that kind of faithfulness today.

> *Many a man claims to have unfailing love, but a faithful man who can find?*
>
> *Proverbs 20:6 (NIV)*

This verse lets us know that most people *think* they are faithful, but few actually are. Born-again believers have, as one of the fruit of the indwelling Spirit, a supply of faithfulness already inside them, ready for use (see Galatians 5:22.) If we, in the New Covenant, lack faithfulness, we are without excuse.

The fact that it is an unusual quality in believers today is a very poor testimony.

PROVING AND PROMOTION

God brings every believer to a local church and pastor, not only for their own spiritual nourishment, but so He can prove their faithfulness. The whole idea of proving, or testing, doesn't always go over very well with Christians. We live in a day where, if people don't see an immediate payoff or reward, they go elsewhere. That kind of unfaithfulness is a sure way to get nowhere.

Those whose minds have been renewed by the Word understand that when God develops people, it is a process that occurs over a long period of time. No one is fully proven by God in a week or even a year. We must resist the fast-food mentality that says, "Give it to me now, and give it to me my way." That just won't work with God. Each of us will have to cooperate with Him and submit to the times of testing that He has ordained.

Pastors also must cooperate with God's work in this area, resisting the temptation to promote people in their congregations too quickly. Just because a person is capable of filling a position does not mean they are spiritually qualified and approved of God for that position. Pastors must be sensitive to the leading of God. Let us make promotion something that is initiated by the Spirit rather than by a ministry vacancy. We will then experience fewer problems and failures among our helpers.

As pastors, my wife and I watched some of our people pass test after test and receive God's promotion. We watched many other people bail-out from the place in which God had set them. We found that only a small percentage of the people who attend churches really want to be pastored and helped. It seems like the majority just attend once in a while so they feel like they're okay with God and won't go to hell. If you suggest to them that they could be a blessing by becoming involved in the ministry, they're gone.

Over the years, I have often been frustrated by the lack of faithfulness I have seen in Bible School graduates. For some reason, their newly acquired education makes them feel exempt from serving another man and proving themselves faithful. They often are obsessed with their own ministry aspirations, failing to understand God's system of proving and promotion. They think that their time of proving was during Bible School. There may indeed have been challenges during school, but let's not confuse *training* with *proving*. God's divine order is *calling, training, proving, promotion*. No one has ever succeeded in getting God to change that order, yet many keep trying.

And if you have not been faithful in that which is another's, who will give you that which is your own?

Luke 16:12

Anyone who wants promotion (all of us should desire God's promotion) should get ready to serve another man. God will call you to serve someone who has already proven themselves faithful. It is quite likely that the person God chooses for you to serve will be a different kind of person than you would have chosen. They may have quirks, or personality flaws. You may think God must not have been aware of some of their shortcomings, but He was; that's why he connected you to them. He'll allow their flaws to rub against your flesh for the purpose of proving you. He wants to see if you can stay put, keep a right heart, and crucify your flesh, until you are no longer irritated by their idiosyncrasies. When you become fully consecrated to the will of God, and develop a heart of faithfulness and loyalty toward those over you, you will arrive at the place where you never want to leave them. Only then can God promote you to another place.

COUNT ON ME

Honor and faithfulness will cause a person to have a reputation for *reliability*. That person will be in high demand by those in leadership because faithful people are not always easy to find. Over the years, I have endeavored to be a faithful help to those to whom God has connected me. If I am helping someone else in ministry or with a project, I want them to be able to put as much weight and responsibility on me as necessary. If they need something, they can call on me and count on me. That is valuable to a leader because leaders know that you can't lean and depend on everyone.

> *Putting confidence in an unreliable person in times of trouble is like chewing with a broken tooth or walking on a lame foot.*
>
> *Proverbs 25:19 (NLT)*

From this day forward, purpose that faithfulness, loyalty, reliability, and honor will be words that others use to describe you.

CHAPTER 17

Honor For Your Spouse

---

*In the same way, **you husbands must give honor to your wives**. Treat your wife with understanding as you live together. She may be weaker than you are, but she is your equal partner in God's gift of new life. Treat her as you should so your prayers will not be hindered.*
1 Peter 3:7 (NLT)

*However, let each man of you [without exception] love his wife as [being in a sense] his very own self; and **let the wife see that she respects and reverences her husband** [that she notices him, regards him, **honors him**, prefers him, venerates, and esteems him; and that she defers to him, praises him, and loves and admires him exceedingly].*
Ephesians 5:33 (AMP)

Some might believe that there are a lot of ways to ruin a marriage, but there's really only one way: dishonor. Unfaithfulness, strife, indifference, abuse, etc. all proceed from a person's failure to correctly value and express that value to their spouse. Honor is a root-level quality of the heart that must forever remain in place in the marriage. It is not a feeling; it is a commitment, a by-product of the love of God.

I have enjoyed a heavenly marriage for over 20 years. Few people have asked me what makes my marriage wonderful, but in case they ever do, I can tell them. It's honor. We make sure we see each other right and treat each other right. We are more in love today than ever, and enjoy every part of our relationship more than ever. A lot of times, we can't keep our hands off each other. I always look forward to coming home because I am honored by my wife. We occasionally endure challenging circumstances, but because of honor, our marriage has not been hard. I cannot imagine a marriage working without honor.

Remember that one meaning of the word *honor* is *heavy*. Honor means that my wife's presence in my life is not a casual thing but a strong, heavy matter. Her words are heavy to me, meaning that I give them the strongest consideration. Her desires are important to me. Neither of us are perfect, and we have our differences, but there are things we would *never* say or do to each other. We do not want to compromise the protective, heavy wall of honor that surrounds our marriage.

LEADING WITH HONOR

God has ordained that the husband be the head of the home. Another word for *head* is *lead*. The husband takes the lead position in the home, which means he must take the lead in showing honor. One meaning of honor is *to exalt to a higher place*. A husband leads honorably by exalting his wife to a higher place, putting her desires and preferences ahead of his own. Honor takes care of her, and puts her first.

Brother Hagin practiced this with his wife. He would often tell about how he cooked breakfast for the two of them, always making sure to give his wife the better piece of bacon. That strip of bacon he gave his wife was an indicator that things were in order in his heart. Why was Brother Hagin able to be exalted to a place of international influence? Because he first exalted his wife to a higher place in their marriage, putting her desires first. His ministry was a success because of honor, and bacon.

> . . . *Treat her as you should so your prayers will not be hindered.*
>
> *1 Peter 3:7 (NLT)*

The scripture above, as well as Brother Hagin's example, reminds us that how we treat our spouse is a *spiritual* issue, not just a natural issue. Peter illustrates the connection between our prayer life and our home life. If we are not seeing results as we ought to in our spiritual life, one of the first things we should do is check the level of honor in our marriage and home life.

I have endeavored to practice these truths in my own marriage. As we have experienced increase over the years, I have tried to put my wife's desires ahead of my own. When I find something she likes, I want to get it for her, even if it means I wait a little longer for something I wanted. Earlier in our marriage, when we finally went from one car to two, I made sure she drove the better one. Over the years, whenever we purchased a newer vehicle, it would become hers, and I would drive the older one. My show of honor to her in this area was rewarded a few years ago when the Lord helped me get a brand new truck that I was believing for. Honor is all over our vehicles, which makes them more fun to drive.

Keep honor in your marriage by putting each other first. Honor in marriage is everything that selfishness is not.

MARRIAGE AND CHILDREN

Some couples make a mistake when children come along. They give their children the place of honor that used to belong to their spouse. Parents, if you still want a marriage when your children are grown and leave home, do not demote your spouse to a lower place. Women sometimes wonder why their husband has lost interest in them. It may be because they have become more of a mother than a wife. Obviously, children need attention, so there is a balance that both husbands and wives must learn and maintain. It should be clear in our homes that after God, our spouse has the highest place of honor.

Parents are right to want to do their best for their kids, but let's understand what really is best for them. If you give your kids the honor of knowing God and serving Him in the church, and then give them the gift of observing a good, strong marriage and family life, you've given them something they will always be grateful for. Never sacrifice your marriage for your children.

MARITAL FAITHFULNESS

Let marriage be held in honor (esteemed worthy, precious, of great price, and especially dear) in all things. And thus let the marriage bed be undefiled (kept undishonored); for God will judge and punish the unchaste [all guilty of sexual vice] and adulterous.

Hebrews 13:4 (AMP)

I once read a good article written by a minister, highlighting the many reasons to avoid having an affair. This minister had used these reasons as a checklist anytime he felt tempted with thoughts of infidelity. Although I had already made the determination to stay faithful to my wife, this article helped solidify in me that an affair was an event I would never be able to afford. As I read the list of consequences, I discovered it was costly from every angle. One of the many heavy consequences on the list was the loss of honor.

Husbands and wives, you have something precious and valuable; something that is worthy of tremendous honor. Never allow honor to dissipate or disappear. Keep honor strong, and your marriage will be strong.

CHAPTER 18

Honor For Children

Fathers, do not provoke or irritate or fret your children
[do not be hard on them or harass them], lest they
become discouraged and sullen and morose
and feel inferior and frustrated.
[Do not break their spirit.]
Colossians 3:21 (AMP)

One of the privileges of parenting is the opportunity to raise children in a culture of honor and watch them thrive in it. When honor is absent, it is a parenting tragedy.

Children, of course, must be taught to honor their parents. While it is a good thing to verbally instruct children in honor, it is an even better thing to give them the example of honor. When children see their Mom and Dad honoring their own parents, and honoring each other, it allows them to take their cue and act similarly. There are also times when a parent can show honor to the child.

Although honor for others often includes submission, I'm not suggesting that the parent is to live in submission to the child. We understand that would be out of order. Honor for children primarily involves showing them their value and importance, and giving them opportunities to rise to the standards and expectations we have set for them. We show honor to a person when we express confidence in their abilities.

There was once a king who heard a request from one of his subjects. The petition made was unusually excessive; everyone who was present gasped in disbelief. The crowd watched as the king took a moment to think, and they anxiously awaited his response, expecting him to dismiss this presumptuous subject. They were startled to instead hear him reply, "The magnitude of your request honors me." When we ask a lot from people, especially our children, it is one way to show honor to them. Of course, wisdom must be exercised, and allowances for mistakes must be made, because impossible demands (especially mixed with wrong words) can discourage a child.

When our kids miss it, we don't beat them down with their mistakes. Instead, we reinforce the fact that we believe they're better than what their present actions are showing. Yes, we bring the necessary correction, discipline, and instruction, but we also help our kids to rise to a higher level by believing in themselves. Psychology will teach these same principles as an intellectual method, but godly honor is not a mental trick. It is initiated from, and received in the heart, and will instill greatness and confidence in the child.

RETAINING DIGNITY

Among the many other character traits and qualities associated with honor, is dignity. Dignity is a sense of self-worth. It must never be taken from a child, yet when a parent, teacher, relative, coach, or other mentor speaks and acts harshly, perhaps out of frustration, dignity can easily be stripped away. Loss of dignity is one of the main reasons why teens look in the wrong places for acceptance and affection. Premarital sex, teen pregnancy, and homosexuality would be at much lower levels if parents would discipline their children while making sure dignity and honor remain intact.

Parents must learn to deal with their children like God deals with His children. Does God sometimes correct us with a strong hand? Absolutely. But, there are things He won't do, like expose your correction to everyone else. The only people in the Bible that Jesus rebuked *publicly* were self-righteous hypocrites. Everyone else was dealt with discreetly.

Of course, younger ones do need to be disciplined on the spot because they won't remember the reason for the discipline later, but when major correction is required for older children, it is best to administer it privately for the sake of their dignity. Here's an example:

Several years ago, when my daughter was just entering her pre-teen years, we let her have a group of friends over for a little party. It was evidently more than she could handle, because she was being quite sassy to her friends, and to her mother and me. Without removing her from the group, I warned her to get the attitude under control. A public warning like that was not out of place because it reminded everyone present of our expectations. When she persisted, I called her away from the group and told her, "It stops now, or else." She chose "else" which involved a prolonged absence from the group and some private punishment. I didn't holler, or threaten to punish her in front of her friends. I administered that penalty privately because I wanted her to focus on the issue of her disrespect, not the embarrassment of her friends being present. I believe our method of discipline that day was a show of honor to her. She has risen up since then and has become a real sweetheart.

CELEBRATING OUR CHILDREN

When Isaac grew up and was about to be weaned, Abraham prepared a huge feast to celebrate the occasion.

Genesis 21:8 (NLT)

There are occasions in the life of a child when it is appropriate to celebrate. These displays of honor toward the child will help develop a heart of honor in the child, and they will rise to a higher level of maturity and responsibility.

One of the ways Jewish people show honor to their children is by having them perform the Bar-Mitzvah ceremony when they are thirteen years old. As a Jewish young man, I had my Bar-Mitzvah, and I have to say it did something to help grow me up. Leading an entire service in Hebrew is no small task. As the Rabbi would mentor me, he continually emphasized that this was a time in my life when I would step into more responsibility – an entrance into manhood. There wasn't just a service, there was also a huge party that followed, all in my honor. My relatives flew in from all over the country for this event. At thirteen, I might not have grasped all that was going on, but the show of honor toward me helped put honor in me.

Other cultures have similar traditions to show honor for their children. These things can be improperly emphasized of course, but I believe a certain amount of celebration for the achievements of our children is healthy. There is no substitute for honor and dignity in our children's lives. They are not optional qualities. Parents, let's teach our children honor, show them honor, and take time to celebrate who they have become.

CHAPTER 19

Honoring Our Elders

Elisha left Jericho and went up to Bethel. As he was walking along the road, a group of boys from the town began mocking and making fun of him. "Go away, baldy!" they chanted. "Go away, baldy!" Elisha turned around and looked at them, and he cursed them in the name of The Lord. Then two bears came out of the woods and mauled forty-two of them.

2 Kings 2:23-24 (NLT)

Noah began to be a man of the soil, and he planted a vineyard. He drank of the wine and became drunk and lay uncovered in his tent. And Ham, the father of Canaan, saw the nakedness of his father and told his two brothers outside. Then Shem and Japheth took a garment, laid it on both their shoulders, and walked back-

ward and covered the nakedness of their father. Their faces were turned backward, and they did not see their father's nakedness. When Noah awoke from his wine and knew what his youngest son had done to him, he said, "Cursed be Canaan; a servant of servants shall he be to his brothers."

Genesis 9:20-25

The natural mind would take issue with these two passages, considering the consequences in both cases to be extreme. I can certainly agree that we should be thankful that we live in the day of grace, instead of the day when judgement came with quick severity. However, these passages are in the Bible by God's design; we must not avoid them, be critical of them, or filter the stories through our own opinions, but must seek for the truths contained within.

These passages leave no doubt as to God's position regarding dishonor toward our elders. Much of the value of the Old Testament is found as God's attitude towards man's actions is revealed. Because He never changes, we know that what irked Him then, still does today. The New Covenant in which we live is full of His love, but because I want to express love back to Him, I am interested in doing what pleases Him, rather than constantly activating His mercy and long-suffering.

Dishonor toward our elders is something that God evidently does not tolerate. Notice in both of these accounts that dishonor was the open door that caused the curse to manifest in the lives of the offenders.

Many think that Elisha just got ticked-off and unleashed his prophetic powers upon these kids, causing the bears to attack them. That is not exactly how these things work. Prophets then and now do what they do by the prompting of the Holy Spirit. If this kind of spiritual power was released any time a minister became frustrated, bears would be eating church members every day!

So what happened? Did Elisha suffer from poor self-esteem? Could he not take a joke? No. God was the one who couldn't take the intense disrespect shown to Elisha by this group of boys. His Spirit came upon Elisha to pronounce judgement, and the curse came upon them swiftly. These boys should have known better. They were probably trained better.

I'm not sure the boys knew that it was the Prophet Elisha they were mocking. It doesn't matter. Elisha was an adult man, and these were adolescent boys. You honor those older than you, period. Respect is always to be shown to our elders. We obviously live in a day where this is not always taught. As a pastor, I have had young adults in my church pass me in the hall and say, "What's up, Dude?" What's up, is a lesson in how to show honor to adults, especially your pastor. Pull up your pants, tuck your shirt in, and realize that you're in the presence of someone who, by virtue of their time on earth alone, is worthy of a show of honor.

So what about Noah's situation? Some don't think it was right that Ham got punished when it was Noah who was passed-out drunk. Most scholars believe however that Noah's drunkenness was accidental, fermentation being an after-effect of the flood that Noah probably didn't yet know about. Where is the dishonor here? It is all over the place. Ham spread the news around the camp that Daddy was drunk and naked. If this happened today, a photo of Noah's backside might have been on social media with the caption "Dad is a party animal!" Ham's brothers teach us honor's lesson here. When a person (especially an elder) misses it, you cover their mistake instead of exposing it. Ham might not have realized that by exposing his father, he was compromising the reputation and honor of the most God-fearing man on earth.

Another lesson is seen here in the story of Noah's family. Children of respected leaders must learn that, although their parents may just be "Mom and Dad" to them, others see them differently. Extra discretion is advised when talking to your friends about your parents. Don't give the impression that they are hypocrites or tell about an argument they had. Parents and leaders are not perfect, and are often dealing with challenging situations that they say nothing about. They make many allowances for the mistakes of their children, and children must sometimes do the same for them.

Some people routinely talk about their elderly parents in a way that shows exceptional disrespect. They speak in a demeaning manner about their parents' physical issues or memory lapses. I've even seen this happen while the parent was present in the room. The child that should be bringing honor to them instead says, "You don't know what you're talking about. You can't remember anything anymore." Do we not realize that the senior years await us all? Do we not believe in sowing and reaping? Do not strip elders of their dignity. It is so important to them. Honor should increase over the course of a life well lived, and should not be stripped away when it is needed the most.

Some of these truths seem to belong to an age gone by, but they must be restored. When I was growing up, I remember going to visit my grandparents. Before getting to their house, my brother and I were cleaned up, dressed up, and trained up in the way we should act. We were told we would have to speak up a little louder than normal so our grandparents could hear us clearly. I appreciate the coaching I received then, and my wife and I did the same with our children when they were younger. When an adult guest or relative is present, children should know that they are not going to have headphones in their ears, they're not going to text or play games, they're not going to look sloppy, and they will not act bored or disinterested. These things are honor issues. We must honor our elders.

CHAPTER 20

Honor For Parents

---

*CHILDREN, OBEY your parents in the Lord [as His representatives], for this is just and right. **Honor (esteem and value as precious) your father and your mother**—this is the first commandment with a promise—That all may be well with you and that you may live long on the earth.*
Ephesians 6:1-3 (AMP)

If people know the Bible at all, they are probably familiar with the commandment to honor Father and Mother. Many know it, but few are serious about practicing it. A closer look at the passage above reveals that there is a direct connection between parental honor and our personal health and prosperity.

There is more to these verses than just teaching little kids to obey their parents (although that is important). There often comes a day when children have the opportunity to reciprocate some of the care their parents gave them in their early years. My earthly father passed away several years ago after a good, long life. When the time drew near for him to leave earth, the Lord began dealing with me about accepting some of the responsibility for the care of my Mother. I began to help with her business dealings, and have managed some of the investments that produce the main part of her monthly income. These activities, especially for the first few years, were a huge drain on my time and energy. I never complained about it though, because it was an act of obedience to the Word of God and the law of honor.

I have often seen people in their older years working minimum wage jobs just to try and survive. It always grieves me to see men and women in their 80's cashing out groceries, instead of relaxing and enjoying life. (I do understand that some older folks work because they want to, not necessarily because they have to.) I want my Mom to live well, drive well, eat well, and be able to do what she desires, as much as possible. Putting forth some effort and even some resources to make that happen is a part of showing honor. I knew that my supply of honor to her would not just work for her benefit, but also to mine. It has. In the years since I have been helping her, instead of being personally drained, our lives have reflected the prosperity of God in every way.

There is a class of people who curse their fathers and do not bless their mothers.

Proverbs 30:11 (AMP)

What class of person is it who isn't interested in doing some things for their Mom and Dad as they progress in age? A dishonorable, low-class person. Some kids spend their whole lives living off their parents and then, when their parents pass off the scene, fight over the little that is left. Don't be a low-life towards your parents. Be a person of honor. Let them know that they don't have to worry about running out of resources and being left alone in their latter days.

KIDS AND PARENTS

We have fun in our home. I'd rather be with my family than with anyone else. Our kids are a constant source of entertainment, and are allowed to goof around with us as long as they do not cross over into dishonor. We have taught our kids to respect our place as parents, and they know that honor is always required. The moment honor is found missing, the fun stops and correction begins.

I have seen families where the parents have given the kids a place equal to themselves. That is out of order and harmful. Children do have equal value with their parents as human beings, but they do not have an equal place in the home.

How can one tell whether honor is in place like it ought to be in the home? Words. How do my children treat my words? Do my words have enough weight in their lives, or do they immediately forget what I tell them to do? Forgetfulness is not a valid excuse, it is a lack of honor. People, including children, remember what is important to them. If you tell your children the family is going out for ice cream after dinner, I guarantee they will remember. Why then, do they not remember to take out the trash? Mom and Dad's words are not heavy enough to them, and are not making the impression that they should. When a parent's words are not making the proper impression, other methods of discipline must be employed that will make an impression.

There's another way that words indicate honor between children and their parents. What kind of words do kids use around their parents? Are there tones of disrespect? Is the parent's presence and opinion discounted in conversation? Are the children too quick to speak, and reluctant to listen? The dinner table is a great sounding board for whether honor is at sufficient levels. If it is not, more training is required.

People today mock the old saying "children should be seen and not heard," and though it could easily be taken to the extreme, there is still an element of truth to it. The presence of adults must be recognized by children. They must be taught that adults have wisdom and life experience that they do not yet have. They should listen and learn more than they should speak, and should never dominate a conversation with adults.

It's not that we are advocating a Gestapo approach to parenting, but many act as though teaching kids honor is some kind of impossibility. Others have listened to too much child psychology, and believe that the principles of honor will somehow hurt their kid's development.

If we will be clear, consistent, and scriptural with our expectations, any family can develop and maintain a culture of honor. All of us have flesh that must be crucified, and all must learn what honor means and how it acts. If children understand honor in the family, they will have an easier time bringing honor into all other areas of their lives.

CHAPTER 21

Honoring Authority

Let every person be subject to the governing author-
ities. For there is no authority except from God, and
those that exist have been instituted by God. Therefore
whoever resists the authorities resists what God has
appointed, and those who resist will incur judgment.
Romans 13:1-2

Whether we are speaking of employers, teachers, parents, or spiritual or civic leaders, the scriptures are clear that we are to receive those in positions of authority as having been appointed by God. He placed them in our lives. Though we may sometimes be privileged to vote for those who govern us, we have no voice or opinion as to the offices themselves. They are God-ordained and must be honored.

We honor the men or women who occupy these places of leadership, and we do so whether or not we agree with how they execute their office. Sometimes leaders (especially elected leaders) perform below our expectations, and it can be tempting to become disgusted with them. When leaders fall short of godly standards, it is okay to feel (and even express) disapproval, but only within scriptural boundaries. Honor must remain in place. It is not right to use our mouths to dishonor their office.

I have lived long enough to experience leaders I liked, and also those I didn't like. I am required by the Lord to respect them all, because the office is worthy of the same respect regardless of who occupies it. I have a big problem when Christians (especially preachers) think it's okay to trash our leaders by stripping them of the respect that their office deserves.

It is okay to respectfully disagree with our leader's policies. It's not okay to loosely run our mouths about someone like our president. I know many who make fun of the president, calling him names, referring to him without the dignity of his title, and even sharing cartoons or unbecoming photographs of him. We can express our disapproval only if we do so in a way that retains the honor of their place.

What's humorous to me is that some of the most outspoken critics of our leaders would stand at attention and break out formal phrases of honor if the same leaders walked into the room. That is hypocritical and disgusting to the Lord.

It is true that some of our leaders have disgraced the offices they stood in, but the fact that they occupied the office in the first place makes a show of honor and respect necessary. Showing honor is an act of obedience to the Lord, not an endorsement of all the policies of a leader.

> *The Lord knoweth how to deliver the godly out of temptations, and to reserve the unjust unto the day of judgment to be punished: But chiefly them that walk after the flesh in the lust of uncleanness, and **despise government**. Presumptuous are they, self-willed, **they are not afraid to speak evil of dignities**.*
>
> 2 Peter 2:9-10 (KJV)

We see from this verse that those who blast the leaders in their lives are not motivated by the Spirit, but are in the flesh, and in rebellion against God. That is a most serious place to be, for those individuals have left a door open in their lives through which the enemy can gain access. Judgement awaits unless they repent, zip their lips, and learn to honor those in positions of authority. We say we are people of faith. Let's use our faith to pray for our leaders. Let us by faith speak good things about them. If we bring dishonorable words to those in positions of authority, we short-circuit the ability of God that is upon them to bring good to our lives.

CHAPTER 22

Honoring The Pastor

Honor for the pastor is an area that should be of interest to every believer, for every believer has been placed under the authority and care of a pastor.

> *The elders who direct the affairs of the church well are* ***worthy of double honor,*** *especially those whose work is preaching and teaching. For the Scripture says, "Do not muzzle the ox while it is treading out the grain," and "The worker deserves his wages."*
>
> 1 Timothy 5:17-18 (NIV)

The responsibilities that every Christian has toward the pastor that God has placed over them can be summed up with one word: *honor*. If we honor our man or woman of God, we will recognize the greatness of their place, understanding that God has placed His anointing upon them for our benefit.

Honor will cause the believer to *properly receive* from his or her pastor. Many do not. Many keep their thoughts elsewhere while he preaches. Some people allow their unsaved friends and family members to influence them to miss church, keeping them out from under their pastor's anointing. There are other people who have a rebellious attitude that refuses to receive and submit. Others still, look down on ministry leaders as weak and unstable, instead of bringing the respect and honor that is due their place.

Thank God for Christians who have learned to receive from the pastor that God has placed in their lives. That however, is not the end of honor. Honor also will reciprocate some things back to the pastor, bringing a level of care to his or her life commensurate with what has been received.

The verses on the previous page speak of bestowing financial and material honor on the leaders of the church. Paul was telling Timothy that a good pastor is worthy of double pay. Whatever a pastor gets paid, it would be appropriate for him to receive just as much, or more, from the blessings that flow to him from his people.

Some of the people in my church received a revelation of this truth and began to do things to help and bless my wife and me. I never asked for these things, but I was grateful to receive them. It was right that they blessed each of us on our birthday and other occasions. It was good that they were always bringing us food, gift cards, and extra personal offerings. Yes, it was good for us, but it was even better for them. Their show of honor toward us was working wonderful things in their own lives. We unapologetically taught our people honor for the pastor's office, and gratefully received the honor shown. We did these things because we cared for our people and wanted the best for them.

> *Not that I seek or am eager for [your] gift, but I do seek and am eager for the **fruit which increases to your credit [the harvest of blessing that is accumulating to your account]**.*
>
> Philippians 4:17 (AMP)

Honor won't look for ways to do less for the pastor, it will look for ways to do more for him. Be sure to refer to your pastor with the honor of his title, receive from the anointing on his life, and reciprocate back with blessings any and every time the Lord puts it on your heart. The church that will honor the pastor in such a way is a church that will likely get to keep their pastor for a very long time.

CHAPTER 23

Honor For The Local Church

I hope to come to you soon, but I am writing these
*things to you so that, if I delay, you may know **how one***
ought to behave in the household of God, which is
***the church** of the living God,*
a pillar and buttress of the truth.
1 Timothy 3:14-15

The level of dishonor toward the house of God has skyrocketed in recent years. I think Christians have heard the phrase *come-as-you-are* for so long that they believe it applies to them. *Come-as-you-are* is an invitation for sinners. Those in the world must come as they are, because nothing they do on their own can improve their lost condition.

Christians are never to come-as-they-are, but must learn to come-as-they-should. They must learn the proper protocol for worship and come having prepared themselves for an encounter with God. Pastors must teach people how to come and how to act at church. Some have thought that the fact that they showed up at all was a major achievement. Friends, it's not good enough for the believer to simply show up. It matters *how* you show up. The scriptures speak vividly to the fact that worship is not an event to be entered into randomly or lightly.

> *Enter with the password: "Thank you!" Make your-*
> *selves at home, talking praise. Thank him. Worship him.*
> *Psalms 100:4 (MSG)*

I could spend all day perusing my bank's website. Although there are some helpful things posted there, what will really help me is to see the information on *my* account. I can't just show up unprepared and get that information; I have to *enter in* to that part of the website with certain protocol. *Then* I get to see everything I want. Just as I bring my user name and password to my banking site, I must make preparation to bring true worship to my local church. It makes all the difference as to what I will be able to receive.

I pastored a church for many years, and taught the people how to come with honor. They learned so well that I didn't realize that people in other churches didn't understand how to act. When I left the church I was leading and started attending other churches, I was shocked at what I saw. Entire rows of kids were playing video games on their phones, *along with their parents*, during the pastor's sermon. People were texting and updating their social media all throughout the service. Those who sat toward the rear of the auditorium felt like they were far enough away to chat with the person next to them. They were far away from honor, for sure.

Parents, don't act like you can't control your kids. Let them know that they must use the bathroom and get their drink of water *before* the service. Tell them they're not going to get up during the service and do those things. It's not right for people to be wandering all around the auditorium or building during a worship service. And no, God is not telling you to get up and go to the back of the room to intercede for the service in warfare prayer. People must learn to focus and concentrate on the service, and we must all realize that our unnecessary movement creates distractions that the enemy can use to keep others from receiving their answers.

But all things should be done decently and in order.
1 Corinthians 14:40

It is the pastor's job to keep the church orderly, and the people must follow. Disorder in worship exists where strong leadership does not. Why are people in many churches today encouraged to bring their food and beverages into the service? Because the pastor has not learned honor for God in a worship setting. He is bringing more honor to the comfort of people's flesh than he is toward the house of God.

*And then I find that you bring your divisions to worship — you come together, and instead of eating the Lord's Supper, **you bring in a lot of food from the outside and make pigs of yourselves**. Some are left out, and go home hungry. Others have to be carried out, too drunk to walk. **I can't believe it!***

1 Corinthians 11:20-21 (MSG)

WE NEGLECT WHAT WE DO NOT VALUE

*Not neglecting to meet together, as is the habit of some, but encouraging one another, and **all the more** as you see the Day drawing near.*

Hebrews 10:25

The scriptures could not be more clear: as we draw closer to the Return of the Lord, meeting more often for worship is a necessity. One very important reason for this is that the corporate anointing (all believers bringing their spiritual supply together) must be strong for the last days' move of God to reach its fulness. There is a sense in which the Return of the Lord depends on the regularity of our coming together for worship. There is no corporate anointing however when we can't get the Body to show up and come together. I have had mornings when half my body wanted to stay in bed. Not very productive. Likewise, if half the people in the church are always absent, the spiritual climate has little chance of developing.

How do believers justify their blatant disobedience of this verse in Hebrews? Believers today are meeting less and less, instead of more and more, and are neglecting public worship. They are neglectful because they do not value corporate worship and do not understand the corporate anointing. They lightly esteem the house of God, and are therefore dishonorable toward their local church.

How often is enough for worship? However many times a week the Lord has led the pastor to schedule services. If it's only once, then be there every single time. If it's two or three times a week, then be there every time the doors are open (of course, I'm not speaking of attending multiple instances of the same service, but different services.) If the pastor schedules a week-long meeting at the church, clear your schedule and come. Any pastor would understand the occasional absence due to vacation, illness, or an unusual scheduling demand, but a Christian should not regularly miss worship.

It is normal in our day for believers to attend church only once or twice a month. These believers may be sweet people but they do not have appropriate honor for the local church. When you sign your kids up for Sunday morning softball league, you are dishonoring God, and will someday regret that decision. It's time to wake up and realize that deception has been at work. If you say you honor God, you will honor the local church. If you say you honor the church, you will not neglect it.

HELPING THE MINISTRY OF HELPS

I have been at churches where I was the guest minister, and when I arrived, no one cared that I was there. The music team was rehearsing, but no usher, ministry of helps, pastor, staff, or volunteer could be found. It's 30 minutes before the service and already I know what kind of service it's going to be, based on the reception at the door.

At some churches, everything is the picture of disorder. *Disorder is the result of dishonor.* When a church is filthy, it is an honor issue. When things are unorganized, it is an honor issue. When there are no greeters, ushers, parking lot workers, children's workers, etc. it is because honor for the local church is missing. When the church is in need of repairs or remodeling year after year, something is wrong. It is not a money issue, it is an honor issue. People will find a way to pay for what is important to them. When I walk into some churches, I know that the people put way more value on their own things than on the things of God.

The local church should be the picture of excellence, order, and honor. I think often of Solomon's kingdom, which was known for a level of excellence that far surpassed any other. Shouldn't the Church of God under the New Testament rate at least as well as an Old Testament kingdom? A non-Jew, the Queen of Sheba, heard about the greatness of Solomon, traveled a great distance to come and see his kingdom, and just about fainted when she saw how well everything was done. Where is that today? People in the world don't honor the Church because so many *in the Church* don't bring honor to it. The world laughs at the Church and dismisses its place of influence. I can't say that I blame them.

Let's grow up, stop playing church, and start having worship. Bring honor to the house of God and God will manifest His honor – His glory – in our midst.

CHAPTER 24

Honor For The Word Of God

Finally, brothers, pray for us, that the word of the Lord
*may speed ahead and **be honored**,*
as happened among you.
2 Thessalonians 3:1

The Body of Christ experienced a mighty revival years ago as believers received a revelation of the power and place that the Word of God is to have in our lives. Bibles, highlighters, and notebooks were everywhere, symbols of this teaching wave. People would write scriptures on note cards and hang them all over their house, in their car, and at work. The Word was everywhere, because honor for the Word was everywhere.

Paul told the saints to pray that the Word might *speed ahead.* Those who watch science fiction movies know what it looks like when a spacecraft makes the jump to light speed. There's a slight pause as all the stars seem to extend, and then *whoosh*, we're gone into another dimension. That's what I think of when I think about the Word speeding ahead. We need to see this kind of spiritual acceleration today, but the Word only speeds ahead when it is honored.

We have fallen back from the days of the teaching revival (which was actually not too long ago.) The voice of society, the constant distraction of media, and the casual attitude of Christians toward the things of God has granted the enemy more headway than we would care to admit. The Word of God is not honored in our day as it ought to be, even by those in the Church. Pastors must not just preach *from* the Word, they're going to have to preach *about* the Word until it is restored to its rightful place of honor within the Church.

When my wife and I were preparing to plant our first church, the Lord spoke something to my heart that I thought was very strange. He gave me a word of instruction regarding my preaching and teaching, saying, "You're going to have to do a lot of teaching about the fact that the Bible is the Word of God." I thought most Christians already believed that, but it didn't take me long as a pastor to see that the majority of believers are not established in that truth.

TALKING THE WORD

Write these commandments that I've given you today on your hearts. Get them inside of you and then get them inside your children. **Talk about them wherever you are, sitting at home or walking in the street; talk about them from the time you get up in the morning to when you fall into bed at night.** *Tie them on your hands and foreheads as a reminder; inscribe them on the doorposts of your homes and on your city gates.*

Deuteronomy 6:6-9 (MSG)

These verses have been part of my life ever since I was a young child. I can still recite a portion of this passage in Hebrew, because every time we came together for worship at my Jewish Temple, this passage was read. It is a foundational passage to the Jewish people, and one that is displayed at the entrance of every Jewish home. Jews have something called a *Mezuzah* (a thin decorative box with a piece of parchment inside) attached to the posts of their front door. On the parchment are scriptures, including this passage. The Jews were the first *word-people* – a group of scripture-confessing, note-taking, word-of-faith believers.

I have been around some religious Jews, and I can tell you that their honor for the Word and the things of God puts most

Christians to shame. They get together with each other, discussing, reciting, and singing the Word. God wants His words *in us* until we are full of the Word. How can we tell if we are full? When the Word starts coming out of our mouths, we are full. When we begin to respond to life's circumstances with God's words instead of our feelings and opinions, we know we are living full of the Word.

Notice in this passage in Deuteronomy that we are to frequently talk about the Word. When the Word is honored, it will be talked about. When I am at Christian gatherings (services, fellowships, etc.) I usually leave grieved at what I hear coming out of the people's mouths. They will talk about the church, the pastor, sports, their hobbies, and new recipes, but not say a word about the Word that was just preached to them.

The Word is the only thing that can renew our minds, it's the only way we know anything about our Heavenly Father, and it is the answer to all of life's problems. We should agree that the Word is worthy of a higher level of honor than anything else, yet its place seems to be neglected by Christians more than anything else.

*I will worship toward Your holy temple and praise Your name for Your loving-kindness and for Your truth and faithfulness; for **You have exalted above all else Your name and Your word** and You have magnified Your* *word above all Your name!*

Psalms 138:2 (AMP)

Honor for the Word, as in other areas, can slip away if effort is not made to maintain it. As I regularly examine myself, there are times when I realize I need to spend more time reading and meditating in the Word of God. It is a dangerous thing for my Word-level to get too low.

Recently, my family and I were reading together from my devotional book, *New Creation Meditations*. After we finished feeding our faith on the scriptures that are in the various chapters, the Spirit of God spoke up on the inside of me and said something that just melted me. He said, "I love hearing my Word read aloud in your home." I realized like never before that He is personally present, listening, and ready to manifest Himself to us when we are giving voice to His Word. The following verse illustrates how God responds when He and His Word are honored and it inspires me to talk about Him wherever I go:

> *Then **those whose lives honored GOD got together and talked it over**. GOD saw what they were doing and listened in. A book was opened in God's presence and minutes were taken of the meeting, with the names of the GOD-fearers written down, all the names of those who honored GOD's name.*
>
> *Malachi 3:16 (MSG)*

CHAPTER 25

Honoring Your Body

---

*For **this perishable body** must put on the
imperishable, and **this mortal body**
must put on immortality.*
1 Corinthians 15:53

Many believers talk about the new body they will receive someday in glory. They assume that our present bodies will be no more, but that idea is not exactly scriptural. The above verse indicates that our present bodies will not be done away with, but rather will take on the properties of immortality. You will have your body, *this one*, forever. Don't worry, the change from mortality to immortality does wonders to a body, fixing anything that is wrong. Neither weight loss nor hair loss will be an issue. When resurrection power hits your mortal body, you will be at your peak, and then some, eternally.

Think for a moment about this transformation that will take place on our way up to meet Him in the air. God will renovate your body with *Himself*. His glory – His honor – will become part of your flesh. Romans 8:11 shows us that we already have the first part of this, our eternal inheritance, as we are indwelled by the Holy Spirit.

> *It stands to reason, doesn't it, that if the alive-and-present God who raised Jesus from the dead moves into your life,* **he'll do the same thing in you that he did in Jesus,** *bringing you alive to himself? When God lives and breathes in you (and he does, as surely as he did in Jesus), you are delivered from that dead life.* **With his Spirit living in you, your body will be as alive as Christ's!** *(MSG)*

If it is God's plan to honor our physical bodies with such a heavenly renovation, how much more should *we* bring honor to our bodies, as caretakers here on earth? When considering the care and honor that God brought to the human body in creation, and the honor he will bring at the resurrection, we should make every effort to keep our bodies in top physical condition.

God is living on earth right now in our bodies. It matters to Him that we keep them in good shape, and it should matter to us. It matters what we put into our bodies. I'm not just referring to things like drugs or tobacco, but also to the food we eat and the beverages we drink. It is poor stewardship and a lack of honor to just let ourselves go physically, and then expect God to somehow keep us well.

My body is part of Christ's body. When factoring in creation, redemption, and the resurrection, He really has more ownership rights than we. If we are married, there is another sense in which our bodies are not our own. My body also belongs to my spouse. My spouse has the right to expect my body to be kept in good shape, and be presented as attractively as possible.

The wife gives authority over her body to her husband, and the husband gives authority over his body to his wife.

1 Corinthians 7:4 (NLT)

Just as demons need the use of a physical body for full expression here on earth, God needs bodies – our bodies – yielded to Him for His expression. When our bodies are well and strong, He is able to flow stronger degrees of His power through us out to the world.

Where you take your body is an honor issue. God doesn't want to go to nightclubs or strip clubs. Take Him where He likes to go. Church is His favorite place.

What you do with your body is an honor issue. What you do sexually is much more than just a physical decision. In this area, The Message Bible once again speaks vividly.

> *There is a sense in which sexual sins are different from all others. In sexual sin we violate the sacredness of our own bodies, these bodies that were made for God-given and God-modeled love, for "becoming one" with another. Or didn't you realize that **your body is a sacred place, the place of the Holy Spirit?** Don't you see that you can't live however you please, squandering what God paid such a high price for? . . .*
>
> *1 Corinthians 6:18-19*

The nature of the flesh would express itself continually through our body. Thankfully, Christ's crucifixion has made possible the crucifixion of our flesh. Saying "No" to the desires of our body is one of the greatest ways we can bring honor to our body. We care for our body best when we discipline it the most. God created your body for a future day of great power and transformation. Until then, we are in charge, and must honor our body as part of the eternal Body of Christ.

> *You were bought with a price [purchased with a preciousness and paid for, made His own]. So then, **honor God and bring glory to Him in your body.***
>
> *1 Corinthians 6:20 (AMP)*

CHAPTER 26

Honor And Excellence

---

*Servants, do what you're told by your earthly masters.
And **don't just do the minimum that will get you
by. Do your best. Work from the heart for your real
Master**, for God, confident that you'll get paid in full
when you come into your inheritance. Keep in mind always that the ultimate Master you're serving is Christ.
The sullen servant who does shoddy work will be held
responsible. **Being Christian doesn't cover up
bad work**.*
Colossians 3:22-25 (MSG)

There's no use arguing about it; Christians are to hold themselves to a higher standard than those in the world. More
should be expected of the believer, for the believer is equipped
for more. Why then, do so many in the Church settle for less?

Those who call themselves atheists actually define Christians as those who have found an excuse to live a life of mediocrity. I normally don't pay any attention to what godless people think, but I realized that they crafted their definition by observing the Church. If I were taking an honest look at the Church from the outside, I'm afraid I would arrive at a similar conclusion.

Honor demands that we strive to be better than we are. We are representing God to the world and must give the world an accurate picture of Him.

When I was in music school, a group of Christian a-cappella singers came on the scene, receiving great acclaim in both the Christian and secular worlds. I will never forget one day, walking down the hall of our jazz department. I heard a recording of one of this group's songs, and was smiling because all the jazz majors were listening to music with Christian lyrics. When I passed the studio where the music was being played, I overheard this comment from the Director of Jazz Studies: "That doesn't sound like any Christians I've ever heard."

What was he saying? His comment revealed that Christians often have a reputation for being underachievers. They often lack the excellence and polish that one finds in the world. Don't we agree that the opposite should be true? We should be leading the way to the top. It used to be that way. Much of society was driven by the Church, because that's where the excellence was.

Having studied music, I can say with authority that most modern musical achievement has its roots in the Church. Ever hear of a guy named J.S. Bach? He revolutionized music in his day and he did it in the Church. He took the current level of excellence through the ceiling and set a new standard for composers everywhere.

More than once, I have heard believers talking about a project or assignment that they had completed half-heartedly. They would say, "Well, it's not very good, but the anointing will make up for it." Where is the scripture that says that? (There is none.) Can you imagine Daniel and his three friends giving that excuse to the King? What if God had that attitude, and redemption only *mostly* worked? True, we should value the anointing and one's heart more than their natural skill, but we must also realize that a lack of excellence is the same as a lack of honor.

Brother Hagin used to tell his son, Pastor Kenneth W. Hagin, "Son, if it's worth doing, it's worth doing right." Anything assigned to us by God is worth doing all the way. Our efforts to bring excellence to our work, craft, and faith is an expression of honor towards Him. Don't just put forth the energy of the flesh, but take time to seek the mind of God and get His plan.

CHAPTER 27

Honor And Humility

Haughtiness comes before disaster,
but humility before honor.
Proverbs 18:12 (AMP)

During the course of my ministry and life, I can think of no area that the Lord has emphasized to me as much as the area of humility. Humility's evil counterpart, pride, is what will be found in our lives, unless a dedicated effort is made to pursue humility. Pride will keep a person from being used of God. It is God's strong desire to be able to exalt, or honor, his called ones in the earth, bringing them to a place of prominence for His glory. But God's exaltation cannot happen where there is self-exaltation.

Some Bible translations use the word *lowliness* instead of humility. I like that word because it gives a good picture of the process of humility. Humility in one's heart is achieved when the flesh and mind have been brought low. It is only in that low position that the person's life can be lifted higher by God.

Many are confused as to what true humility looks like, but it can be easily understood by contrasting it with pride. Pride is the error of believing lies about yourself. Humility, on the other hand, is believing the truth about yourself. In ourselves, we can do nothing, we know nothing, we have nothing, we are nothing. In Christ, we can do all things, we have all things, we know all things, and have become all things. Humility glorifies God, recognizing that all the good in our life is a result of our being in Christ. Pride looks at the good in our life and mistakenly assumes credit for it. Humility means that we agree with the spiritual realities about ourselves as taught in the Bible.

Humility increases one's capacity for honor. The life of humility is the life that is able to see and understand when honor is due, and recognize those to whom it is due. If everyone could see these things, all would walk in honor instead of just a few, but pride has a blinding effect on the spirit of man. It is God's desire that many more of His children decrease in pride, becoming able to clearly see honor's path. Then their lives will be positioned for the increase of God.

True humility and fear of the Lord lead to riches, honor, and long life.

Proverbs 22:4 (NLT)

The humble life will not only direct proper honor toward God, it will also position that life to receive honor from God. God can bestow His honor and glory upon the life of the humble. To the proud, God can only stand in opposition. The humble person will be around a long time, will be blessed, and will receive ever-increasing measures of God's honor back into their life. It is true in the Kingdom of God, that the one who desires to go up must first go down. The life that would be raised up and exalted must first be lowered: emptied of self and filled up with God.

CHAPTER 28

Honor Is Enough

In the classic movie *Gone With The Wind*, there is a scene where the conflicted Ashley Wilkes is confronted by Scarlett O'Hara, who wants him to leave his wife for her. Ashley agrees that his natural affections are probably stronger for Scarlett, but he declines her advance, determined to stay faithful to his wife. Here's how he explained his decision:

"Even if feelings of love aren't reason enough to stay [with his wife], *honor alone is enough*."

Honor is enough. It is all the reason we need to do the right thing, every time.

Asking "What would honor do?" is a safe consideration when making decisions, for our guide, the Holy Spirit, will always lead us according to what is honorable and right. When it looks like there is every reason to abandon something or someone, but it just isn't the honorable thing to do, we are to say the same thing Ashley said: "Honor alone is enough."

CHAPTER 29

Honor's Reward

Those who honor me I will honor . . . .
1 Samuel 2:30

Honor is everything to me. Honor for God, honor for my spouse, honor for my kids, honor for others, honor for my pastor, honor for myself, etc. As I have learned the principles of honor, I have endeavored to practice them in my life. I have missed it at times of course, but the more I have seen about this subject in the Word of God, the more I have been inspired to become a man of honor. These truths about honor seem to resonate in my heart like nothing else.

If honor's only payout was the knowledge that a measure of Christ-likeness was achieved, it would be worth it. If our reward were all reserved for Heaven, it would still be okay. But there are rewards here on earth associated with honor that are as precious as anything in this world.

I have discovered this truth: *honor's reward is honor.*

When we bestow honor, we receive honor. When we show honor *to* God, whether directly or by honoring His represen-tatives here on earth, we receive honor *from* God. I know of nothing more powerful than receiving honor from God.

There have been times when I have reaped honor's reward in ways that are powerful and overwhelming. To borrow a phrase from the world, God has *blown me away.* He has done things for me that have touched me so deeply that I just fall on my face before Him and worship. I will say to Him, "Lord, You have honored me." He always replies, "I told you that if you would honor Me, I would honor you." I know He'll always answer me that way because it is scriptural. I never tire of hearing it.

He has honored me financially. He has brought homes, cars, and other items to us at different times that were exceedingly, abundantly, above all we could ask or think. Those things hap-pen because I honor Him financially. He can have anything of mine at any time because He gave it all to me to begin with.

He has honored me with His anointing to minister, some-times in measures so strong, I can hardly stand up under it. He honors me with His anointing because I honor His anointing.

He has honored me by blessing my family. I have given my life to bless His family.

He honors me with His presence, because I honor His presence.

When I give Him all the glory, He gives me measures of His glory.

Honor is my reward. I am an honor addict. No, not an ego addict. I don't mean that at all. Nor do I talk about the things God has brought into my life to place inappropriate emphasis on my possessions or works. It's *His* goodness that blesses my socks off, not mine. I draw attention to what I have done only to show that doing our part is necessary.

Because I have had a taste of honor's reward, I can tell you that whatever price you have to pay to do right will be well worth it. Honor will eventually be received back into your life. The measures of glory that await you are a heavy weight (in a good sense) that you will carry around with you all of your days. If you don't have honor, you don't have anything. If you lose honor, you've lost everything.

Rest assured that our life of honor will not be forgotten by God. Reward always follows honor.

CHAPTER 30

Final Thoughts

Most would probably agree, not everything in this book has been gentle, complimentary, and positive. Some parts have been corrective in nature, but all parts have been motivated by the love of God. My prayer is that you will make adjustments, positioning yourself for honor's reward. My desire is that the Body of Christ will respond, allowing God to pour out His power in a stronger measure than we have ever seen.

All our efforts will be worthwhile when we experience the highest degree of His honor – in eternity.

And the city had no need of the sun, neither of the moon, to shine in it: for the glory of God did lighten it, and the Lamb is the light thereof. And the nations of them which are saved shall walk in the light of it: and the kings of the *earth **do bring their glory and honor into it.***

Revelation 21:23-24 (KJV)

Appendix:
Pastors And
Traveling
Ministers

APPENDIX 1

Pastors And Traveling Ministers

In my years of full-time ministry, I have spent about half my time traveling, and half as a senior pastor. I certainly don't claim to know everything, but I do have some perspective gained from time spent in both fields of ministry. There is much to say about the pastor and traveling minister where honor is concerned.

Many dynamics come into play here, and this is a touchy subject for some. There are pastors who have had bad experiences with traveling ministers, and have consequently adopted policies in order to protect themselves and their church. Some traveling ministers have been taken advantage of by pastors, and therefore feel they must set certain requirements for the safety of their own ministry. The amount of distrust that exists in some places between churches and those in traveling ministry is saddening.

Pastors are often inundated with phone calls, emails, and letters from ministers looking to schedule meetings in churches. The whole idea of the traveling minister is something that some pastors wish would just go away. The traveling minister is necessary however, as the church member will never receive all that he or she needs from just the pastor. God placed all the gifts in the Body because they are all necessary for the development of the Body. The pastor is the one who regularly feeds, but those who occupy other offices must be brought in for special times of instruction and impartation. To illustrate, I usually eat what comes from the grocery store, but there are special times when I go to a restaurant. Both types of meals are a blessing, and between the two I get all the food I need.

Pastors, you must be willing to deal with the traveling minister, and have them in at least once in a while to help mature the saints. Let's do things right and bring honor to this relationship.

The Lord spoke something to my heart soon after my wife and I planted our first church. I was thinking about the possibility of bringing in our first guest minister when I heard these words in my spirit: *If you will honor the ministers I bring to you, I will see to it that the very best come to your church.* I don't think anyone would argue that what I heard that day was in agreement with the teachings of scripture.

We immediately began putting that word into practice, making sure to do our very best to honor the ministers we had in. Although our church was still very young, we had some of the top ministers in the land preach for us. Some of the most powerful services I have ever enjoyed in my life were meetings in my own church. Why? Honoring the traveling minister was something we took seriously.

LEARNING TO PREPARE

I believe the most helpful thing we did in this area was to properly prepare our congregation for the meetings. Guest ministers were a special event for our church. Just as soon as the meeting was booked, I would let the people know about it. There were three main purposes for this.

First, people's calendars fill up quickly and for some, anything other than a Sunday morning service requires advance planning. Our people were encouraged to arrange their schedules to make preparation for the meetings. We would usually print up some kind of invitation to the meetings to give to our people so they could invite others. We found that if they took these home, it also helped keep the upcoming meetings in their own thoughts.

A second reason why we gave as much notice as possible to our people was so they could prepare their giving. I would always rehearse what the Lord spoke to me about honoring the guest minister, and would remind everyone that one way honor is shown is through giving. We would prepare for the expenses of the meeting ahead of time so that we could concentrate on giving, not paying bills, when the time came for the meetings. We would encourage our people weeks ahead of time to check their hearts and set a goal for their giving in the meetings. We wanted to send our ministers away with as big an offering as possible, because money talks. It can say loudly, "You are honored here at this church."

Some pastors choose to give an honorarium to the minister instead of an offering. There are certain times when that may be appropriate, but as a usual thing I like receiving offerings for the minister. Offerings allow the people to directly respond to what they received in the service. When people are well taught, offerings are an easy setting in which God's multiplication can occur, and it doesn't limit the amount that the minister can receive.

I despise it when I encounter pastors who are concerned about the traveling minister getting too much money. It's as though they believe they're in competition with the traveling minister for the congregation's money, the pastor trying to keep as much of it in-house as possible. That's not just dishonorable, it's ungodly, stingy, and a huge display of unbelief in the principles of God's Word. Just as ungodly though, is the traveling minister who tries to suck every dollar he or she can out of the local church, using every means imaginable (we'll discuss this a bit more in an upcoming section.)

The third reason why we would give advance notice to our congregation, continually announcing the meetings, was so they had time to apply their prayers and faith to the meeting. When the day finally came for the services to start, expectation was high and the results were tremendous.

Sadly, there are many congregations who show up on Sunday to see their pastor introduce a guest minister they didn't even know was coming. One sentence in the bulletin might have been all the notice they had. Maybe not even that. What kind of meeting do you think they'll have under those circumstances? The people were completely unprepared and it's really the fault of the leadership (if indeed the meeting was booked ahead of time.)

Some churches don't say anything about guest ministers because they don't want to add any burden to the people by talking about an extra offering. Pastors get afraid that if they say anything about money people will leave. Those pastors are robbing their flock by not giving them the opportunity to take the responsibility that's theirs. They should begin training their people in this area from the Word, and in most cases, the people will joyfully respond.

Other churches fill their calendars with so many special events each month that the people couldn't possibly make appropriate preparation for each one. Those churches should consider being more selective in their scheduling, and they will find themselves more effective in ministry.

It does occasionally happen that a minister is booked at the last minute and advance notice cannot be easily given to the congregation. If the people have learned to prepare their hearts for *every* service, all will be well. A few times over the years, we had ministry guests whom we booked at the very last minute. Sometimes they were holding a date for another pastor who kept them waiting so long for a confirmation that they suddenly found themselves with an open date in our area. In those cases, I would receive a special offering at the end of the service for them, but since the people didn't have time to make advance preparation, I would tell them to pledge any additional amount they wanted beyond what they had on hand. We usually specified a two or three week time frame to receive this delayed offering. I would give the minister the offering that had come in that day before he left, and would send the rest when it came in.

Pastors and traveling ministers must remain honorable toward each other. The following sections provide even more detail to help safeguard from distrust and avoid dishonor.

APPENDIX 2

7 Tips To Help Ministers Stay Honorable And Not Lose Their Peace Over Money

Although most ministers are peace-loving individuals, tensions arise when poor communication or questionable practices are present. When ministers do find themselves in sticky situations, it is often a problem that revolves around money. Here are some practical steps to take, so the pastor and traveling minister can avoid stressing each other out.

1. Pastors should take the initiative and be up-front regarding finances. Let the guest minister know how things work at your church so there are no unpleasant surprises. The verses below suggest that we should develop the habit of thinking ahead of time about potential areas of conflict. What effect will my actions have on the congregation? Will this hurt the guest minister? Am I sowing a seed that will return an unpleasant harvest to my own life?

*Repay no one evil for evil, but **give thought to do what is honorable in the sight of all**. If possible, so far as it depends on you, live peaceably with all.*

Romans 12:17-18

We create problems for ourselves when we do things that appear sly or underhanded. For example, if the pastor announces from the pulpit that an offering is being received for a guest minister, then it is wrong to subtract expenses from it. One hundred percent of what comes in should go to the guest minister because that was implied when the offering was received. I have known a few pastors who deducted expenses from the minister's offering, but everyone clearly understood the arrangement ahead of time. It is dishonorable to tell a minister "We will receive offerings for you," only to later surprise him with an itemized list of meeting expenses that were deducted from the offering.

2. The pastor should give the traveling minister his offering and other funds due him (travel expense reimbursement, if applicable) as soon as possible, preferably before he leaves town. Some churches meet in temporary facilities, and offerings are not able to be processed on the premises. In those cases, the pastor should inform the guest minister of the church's accounting time frame, so the minister knows when he can expect to receive his check. Don't allow the minister to leave wondering if and when he will ever see

the offering. I know of some churches that take months to get the offering to the guest minister. What are they doing with the money that whole time? Did they spend it, and are now trying to save up for it again? That's beyond dishonorable; it's stealing.

3. If a pastor invites a traveling minister to come to his church, it should be expected that the church will pay the expenses. Why would I, as a pastor, invite a guest to travel to my town and then expect him or her to pay for the trip? The business world usually sets a better example than that. I have seen how the world rolls out the red carpet for its VIP's. They stay in the penthouse suite and get the key to the city. As the Church, let us at least not leave the ministers we invite in holding the bill for the expenses.

We would sometimes book traveling ministers when they were already in the region, ministering for other churches. Although the burden for travel expenses wasn't officially placed on us, I would offer to pay my part. Usually, I would call the neighboring pastor who had originally booked the minister, and offer to split the expenses. Was I doing this because I had tons of extra cash in the account? No. I did these things because they were right to do. If honor demands it, I know there will be a supply for it. I never wanted the traveling minister paying his own expenses, regardless of how the ministry engagement was booked.

4. If a traveling minister *asks* to come minister at a church, he should not assume the church will pay his expenses. Sometimes, I know I will be traveling in an area and will make contact with a church that has never expressed interest in my ministry. I will tell them "I can come at no expense to you." After all, I'm the one *asking* to come; I wasn't invited. Sometimes they are gracious and will pick up my hotel bill, buy my meals, or even pay a portion of my travel. Although I appreciate and gratefully receive their show of honor, it's not *expected* on my part.

5. The traveling minister must be sensitive to the operation of the local church. If a traveling minister has never been a pastor, he or she may not realize how much money it takes to host a guest with honor. It is not unusual for the church to spend a considerable amount (sometimes as much, or more, than is received in the offerings) on expenses for the guest minister.

I have heard pastors of smaller churches comment that after having certain guest ministers in, it took them six months to recover financially. This was not just because of expenses, but because of some of the unethical practices of the guest minister (see later section: *Mistakes the Traveling Minister Makes*.) Leaving a spiritual deposit in the local church should always be the main goal of the traveling minister, not seeing how much money they can extract.

6. Sometimes meetings are booked as ministers fellowship together in public places (at a ministry conference, for example.) It is not always appropriate in such settings to discuss details like travel expenses. In those cases, the traveling minister should follow-up to confirm (rather than just assuming) that their travel will be covered by the host church. Again, I believe it's even better if the pastor takes the lead in this area. If your church can't take care of all the expenses, get in touch with the minister and tell them what you are prepared to do. The traveling minister will appreciate the communication.

7. Both the traveling minister and the pastor must develop and exercise faith in order for this type of ministry to function as it should. There is a divine supply for special meetings and conferences, but that supply does not flow when faith is not exercised. For some churches, having anyone in seems like a stretch on the finances. And, some traveling ministers feel as though they're barely making ends meet. Too often, faith is absent, replaced by pressure, suspicion, and fear. When all parties bring faith, they will enjoy watching God make up any difference, and the financial needs will all be met.

The Honorable Traveling Minister

Traveling from church to church is anything but glamorous. Along with any other challenges the traveling minister faces, he has the responsibility to try and leave each church having been a blessing to both the church and the pastor. This doesn't always occur. Sometimes the traveling minister does all he is supposed to, but his ministry is not received. Other times, the traveling minister creates his own problems by the things he does and says. The following pages contain guidelines to help the traveling minister leave a church in better shape than he found it. It is not a good thing when the pastor is overly excited to get the traveling minister back to the airport!

GIVE ME LIBERTY! (OR I'LL TAKE IT ANYWAY)

Regardless of the traveling minister's call, gifts, stature in the Body, or opinion of himself, he is *always* subject to the pastor of the local church. In most cases, that pastor has spent years caring for the sheep. He knows his people better than anyone else. The traveling minister might occupy an office that carries a stronger degree of anointing than that of the pastor (such as the apostle or prophet), but no minister has a higher place of authority in the local church than the pastor of that church.

Those who are true pastors are very cautious with who they have in to minister, and rightfully so. If a pastor invites or allows me to come to his church, I must be respectful of his place. When I meet up with the pastor at his church, I am listening closely for any instructions he might have for me: anything he might want me to do or not do in his pulpit. If he says nothing, I will usually ask, "Is there anything I need to know?" It's not that I feel a need to know all the details about his members (on the contrary, I'd rather not know a lot of details about the people who might be present), rather, I need the pastor to know that I respect his place. If there are boundaries, I want to know them; It's not right for me to go beyond the liberty he gives me.

Often, without my asking, a pastor will say something like, "Please minister whatever God gives you. We're hungry and open." That pastor just gave me liberty in his pulpit to follow God. I like that best. However, sometimes they will say, "Please stay off this subject" or "Don't say a lot about such-and-such." Those are instructions I must obey, and I will do my best to flow with God within those parameters. What if I feel led otherwise? That is not an option. I am not free to be led beyond the boundaries that the pastor has set. God will not violate the pastor's authority in his own church by leading me to disobey. If I feel as though I am supposed to say or do something, and cannot get the pastor's blessing to do it, God will not hold me accountable. I will be held responsible however, if I choose to ignore the pastor's instructions, violating his directives and undermining his authority before all his people. That pastor would be well justified in never having me back.

Pride would say things like, "Well, they shouldn't have had me in if they didn't want me to follow the leading of the Spirit" or, "They don't honor my gift there" or, "I'm going to obey God, no matter what anyone else says." Go ahead, and watch what a huge mess will follow. Honor, humility, and faith won't say those kind of things, but will follow instructions without needing to know all the reasons why. More important than the word that we preach is the fact that we can recognize and stay in our place.

I can recall a few of my road meetings where the pastors gave me specific instructions regarding what to do or preach. I wasn't excited about their requests because I personally would have chosen to go a different direction. What does a traveling minister do if this happens? He or she can follow the pastor's instructions or ask to be released from the meeting. In the case of my meetings, I was free to be led, but only within the boundaries that had been given me. I reminded myself that the pastor knew his church much better than I. Though I had initially been disappointed with what I considered to be restrictions, I went ahead and submitted to the pastor. We all believed for big results and were not the least bit disappointed.

My willingness to be flexible and obedient to these pastors (who didn't know me very well at the time) was so important. By honoring them, I also honored God, and He in turn honored us by manifesting Himself in the meetings. I felt like I was able to establish a level of trust with these pastors. I suspect that, should I be invited back, I will be offered even more liberty. Respecting the place of the pastor in the local church is a matter of honor.

There is something to be said to the pastor in this discussion of liberty in the pulpit. Pastors are sometimes guilty of trying to control their church so tightly that they do place unnecessary restrictions on the visiting minister. Unless God deals with you to limit their ministry to one area, let the Lord lead them to minister however He desires. The fact that the visiting minister doesn't know your crowd as well as you can be a good thing, and it's often amazing how God orchestrates the ministry content to bring exactly what is needed.

Mistakes Pastors Make With Guest Ministers

The next several pages speak about common mistakes that are made by those in ministry. These points are not meant to arouse a fault-finding spirit in the reader, but are meant to help erase dishonor in ministry. The reader may recognize some of these practices in pastors or other ministers they know, but if you have never walked in the minister's shoes, you are not in position to judge. Ministry situations are often multi-sided, and only one side may be visible to those looking on. As we read on, the person we should be inspecting is ourself. Many situations in life mirror these ministry situations.

MISTAKE #1: BEING UNTEACHABLE AND UNRECEPTIVE

Pastors must remember to be receptive and teachable. Many times, I have been in meetings that were attended by pastors who sat there expressionless; they had obviously forgotten how to receive in a service. Pastor, the guest minister is there to minister to you, as well as to your people. None of us knows everything, and we all must be perpetual students of the things of God. Because the traveling minister is often directed to specialize in their ministry, they may have great proficiency in certain areas. *Learn something from them*, and be impressed by their ministry, not intimidated by it. Give them an "amen" once in a while as they are ministering. Do not fall into the trap of sitting there, comparing their ministry with yours; and, don't feel like you have to act as though you already know everything they are preaching (although you may.) Pastors must themselves practice what they teach their own people: faith gets excited every time it hears the truth.

MISTAKE #2: RE-PREACHING THE GUEST MINISTER'S MESSAGE

It is right for the pastor to show excitement about what the guest minister has preached. However, many pastors miss it when they start re-preaching the guest minister's message right after he finishes. If the preacher was anointed, that anointing is working in the people. Let them leave hearing the voice of the guest minister. Build on his message the next Sunday if you want, but right after the guest minister finishes is not the right time. Although likely unintended, getting up and amending the message right after the minister finishes is a show of dishonor. The people might think that the pastor found the message lacking in some way, and is trying to fix it.

A guest minister sometimes brings something to a service that is not normally there. Consider this example: If a friend asked me to lunch and picked me up in a brand new sports car, I would really enjoy the ride to the restaurant. If my friend pulled up to the door of the restaurant and said, "I have to use the bathroom right away, you park the car," I would gladly oblige. However, I would be very tempted to not just park the car, but drive it around the block a few times. It's something fun that I'd really like to try out. When there is an extra-good service, pastors have to discern whether it's right to get up and take the congregation around the block a few more times, or if it's really best to just put the service in park.

MISTAKE #3: USING UP THE GUEST MINISTER'S MINISTRY TIME

Churches typically have a lot going on. Sunday morning is usually the time for most of the announcements and other church business. It's also a time that guest ministers come.

We must not be ritualistic with the different segments of a service; always singing the same number of songs; always preaching a sermonette before the offering; always having testimonies, ministry to the sick, prayer, etc. These things are not inherently wrong, but when a guest minister has been invited in, it's time to start carving away any elements that are not absolutely necessary. As a pastor, I loved changing things up in the service because it helped to keep people out of ruts, mindlessly going through the motions.

When we would have guest ministers in our church, we would usually slim down all the other parts of the service: perhaps cut a song or two out of praise and worship; have the people greet each other without taking as much time as they normally would; leave out announcements that could wait until next week, etc. When I received the offering, I would maybe read a verse, but that's about it. My goal was to get the service turned over to the ministry guest as soon as possible. I wanted the guest minister to have all the time he or she needed. These are practical issues, but also honor issues. Can I really say I am honoring the guest minister if I don't give him or her adequate time in the service?

People are used to their own pastor's ministry, but are not as familiar with the guest minister from whom they are receiving. Likewise, the guest minister may be unfamiliar with a new congregation. It can take several minutes in some cases for the minister to warm-up and feel like he is connecting with the people. Allow time for this; it is important that a real ministry connection occur. Don't take away from the substance of what the guest minister came to deliver by not respecting his or her ministry time.

I have seen pastors take 30 minutes to receive the offering and then invite the guest minister up, telling them before the congregation, "Take all the time you need, brother." That may sound honorable, but it is not realistic. The babies in the nursery don't know how to make the adjustment for a longer service. And, the people are used to dismissing at their usual time. They may act polite in an extended service, but they probably aren't receiving like they would have had the minister taken the service earlier. On the other hand, if there is only one service scheduled with a guest minister, pastors are wise to prepare the people ahead of time for the possibility of going a little bit longer. Knowing in advance can make a great difference to people, and informing them shows that you honor their time.

One of the main reasons why pastors take up so much time in the service is pride. They want the guest minister (and any visitors who came to hear the guest minister) to know that they indeed can preach, too. Let's put away such childishness and be honorable with the pulpit time of the guest minister.

Mistake #4: Tapping Into the Guest Minister's Anointing

Pastors sometimes spend too much time ministering during a guest minister's service because of the anointing that is present. When you combine the heightened expectation of the congregation with the anointing on the life and ministry of the guest minister, there can be a tangibility in the service that is greater than normal. The pastor must recognize that this anointing is there for the guest minister to use, not for the pastor himself to use. The pastor might step into the pulpit to make announcements and suddenly sense the anointing to heal, pray, preach, and prophecy. It's not yours today. Get it turned over to the guest minister and let him tap into it.

I once watched a service featuring a well-respected traveling minister. The pastor at this church got up to take care of some business, and then proceeded to pray and prophecy for at least 15 to 20 minutes. Most people would say, "Wasn't that wonderful?" But it wasn't wonderful because it wasn't honorable. The pastor finally turned the service over to the guest minister, who came to the pulpit and exclaimed, "Well, there's really nothing left for me to do now. You've done it all already." Although the pastor probably didn't mean it, the extra time he spent in the pulpit was a show of dishonor to that traveling minister.

MISTAKE #5: NOT RESPECTING THE TRAVELING MINISTER'S PREPARATION TIME

When a minister is endeavoring to minister by the Spirit, preparation time is increased, and the budgeting of time becomes all the more important. Pastors and traveling ministers must both be aware of this dynamic and be disciplined with how they use their time. Although every minister should learn to wait upon the Lord before he ministers, many prepare their message and do little else.

Traveling ministers may preach some of the same sermons everywhere they go, but they must still take time to prepare their heart. I have heard stories of some guest ministers who were preaching every evening in a city, but would go to the movies every afternoon. Ministers who operate in that fashion are not showing honor to the office in which they stand. They also are dishonoring the congregation to whom they are ministering and the pastor who invited them.

We live in an era where God is desiring to move supernaturally in greater ways than many of us have seen before. Heart preparation is essential, and it takes time. Pastors can make the mistake of borrowing from the guest minister's preparation time as they spend time fellowshipping together. Always defer to the wishes of the guest minister. Don't keep the conversation going eternally. The guest minister may not want to be impolite by asking, "Can I please get back to my room?" so he stays longer than he wants to. It is true, pastors don't always have people they can talk to. The guest minister is a valuable resource to the pastor, but ultimately he is in town to help the whole congregation, not just the pastor. Honor him by making sure he has enough preparation time during the day.

MISTAKE #6: NOT RESPECTING THE TRAVELING MINISTER'S REST TIME

Traveling can be tiring. Ministry can be tiring. When you do both together, it can be physically exhausting. Pastors must account for the toll that traveling and ministering takes on the body of a guest minister. I have spent time around some very seasoned ministers who traveled extensively. Some of them were in their golden years. There were times when I could see fatigue affecting them. They didn't say anything, but I wondered why no one else seemed to notice, and why the people hosting the meeting didn't suggest we let them get back to the room to sleep instead of keeping them up at the dinner table for hours.

No matter how anointed someone is, they are still mortal. Their time and strength is not unlimited. Do we not realize that keeping them up an extra two hours at night means that it will take them longer to recover from their trip when they get home? Honor doesn't presume that it's acceptable to borrow a person's strength from their family that is waiting for them back home. Let the guest minister be the one to say, "I want to stay here and visit a while longer." The pastor's goal should be for the guest minister to leave refreshed, not drained.

MISTAKE #7: FAILING TO RECOGNIZE AND RESPECT THE GUEST MINISTER'S EXPERIENCE, BACKGROUND, AND REVELATION

The pastor and guest minister must each value the life experiences of the other. I have been at the table with visiting ministers who were people of great anointing and experience, and I watched as the host pastor spent the whole time preaching to us. I guess he wanted to make sure we all knew how much he knew. He spent the evening advertising that he *didn't* know one of the most important things: honor. I wanted to reach over, grab him with both hands and say, "Shut up. Don't you realize who you're sitting with?"

Once, a person struggling with physical sickness was able to get a 20-minute appointment with Brother Hagin. The man started the meeting by talking about his physical condition, and never stopped talking. After the 20 minutes were up, Brother Hagin stood up and said, "Well, I have to go now. Goodbye." The man never received anything, even though the man who knew the answers was sitting right across from him. That was a blatant display of dishonor.

Realize who you are with, and show honor. Don't do all the talking. As Dad Hagin was fond of saying, "You already know everything you know." Be a learner. Be a good student, even if the person is younger than you. Get to know the ones you are privileged to visit with. Read their books. Listen to their recordings. Then ask questions and listen.

MISTAKE #8: NOT MAKING THE GUEST MINISTER FEEL WELCOME

Pastors are tremendously busy people. We understand that. When I travel, I don't expect the pastor to baby-sit me. I enjoy the pastor's fellowship, but it doesn't bother me if he doesn't have extra time to visit with me. What should be important to pastors is that the guest minister feels welcomed and honored. There are ways to accomplish this without breaking the bank.

When I was a pastor, I had a policy concerning guest ministers. No guest minister at our church would ever show up to an empty hotel room. By empty, I mean no acknowledgment at all from the church that brought him in. We would always have a nice gift basket in the room for the minister. Not just two bananas and a bottle of water sitting on the desk, but something wrapped up real nice. We would find out what they liked and shower them with goodies.

What if they can't eat it all, or it's just a one-day meeting? That's irrelevant. It's not the food, it's the heartfelt show of honor. It's something that says, "We are so excited that you're here. You and your ministry are so special to us." I don't care if they take one bite of an apple and leave the rest of the items wrapped up for the hotel cleaning staff to take home. I do care that we send the message that we are thrilled to have them.

When it was time to feed the guest minister, I would find out what they liked, and made sure they ate the best of the land. It didn't always have to be the most expensive to be great. Was I trying to impress him? No, I wanted to honor him. There's a difference between putting on a show, and genuine care and honor.

SAVED BY A GIFT BAG

I often marvel about an experience in prayer that I had. A pastor, for whom I had preached many months earlier, had a medical emergency which easily could have been a fatality. The day prior, and the day of his physical attack, I had a burden of prayer and found myself interceding for someone who's life was in danger. When I later heard about his situation, I sensed that at least part of what I was praying about that day involved him. Thankfully, the situation turned out positively.

What was so interesting, was that the Lord alerted *me* (along with others, I'm sure) to pray for this minister, whom I didn't know very well on a personal level (of course, I was glad to be used to bring a spiritual supply to his situation.) I figured there were others who were much more closely associated with him than I. When I asked the Lord about this, He reminded me of something that might seem strange: the gift basket that was in my hotel room when I went to his church. These pastors went out of their way to make me feel extra-special. My family was with me on this trip, and they gave a nice gift bag to each of my kids. When we came in the room, we were so blessed and touched by their show of honor toward us.

I learned a great lesson when I saw how this family's honor toward me created a spiritual connection, allowing me to return a tangible supply back into their lives from across the country. Again, I'm sure that others were also used of God to bring a supply of help to this minister at a time when he was unable to help himself. My point here is that a gift basket can save your life. Honor can save your life.

When pastoring, we always made sure our guest ministers were in a comfortable hotel. We would sometimes go to the hotel ahead of time and ask to see the rooms. If a suite was available and was within our means to purchase, we would reserve the suite. Who rents the suites in hotels? Important people. I wanted our guest ministers to know that we saw them as important. Why? So they'd step into the pulpit in the fulness of their office, knowing that there was a room full of receivers who honored their ministry. People would sometimes ask why the meetings at our church were top-shelf. This is why.

It's not always easy for the traveling minister to leave their family and home to go on the road. When they came to my church, I wanted them to feel like they hadn't.

MISTAKE #9: POOR COMMUNICATION AND LYING

We've already talked about financial communication. Most traveling ministers would appreciate *any* communication from the pastor, or his representatives.

As has been said, pastors receive many meeting requests from traveling ministers. As a pastor, my mailbox, voice mail, and email received a constant flow of such communication. If I did not know anything about the minister's background (what Bible School he went to, or what church he traveled out of), I would likely not respond at all. If the minister had gone to the same school as I, he would be invited to forward his ministry information to my office for review. I only booked meetings as I was led of the Spirit.

If someone I knew *personally* made contact with me, I would always try to respond personally. Even if I was not led to have them minister for me (or the dates just didn't work), I'd still respond, as a matter of honor. I ignore telemarketers, junk mail, and junk email. I *don't* ignore friends and fellow ministers, because I was taught that ignoring people is rude. I understand that in today's culture, where people are flooded with communication, it has become acceptable not to return texts, calls, emails, etc. Remember though, our culture knows nothing about honor. When a respected minister gets in touch to inquire about ministering at your church, don't make him wonder if the message ever reached you. Respond. It's the honorable thing to do. They're adults; they can handle hearing "Thank you, but not at this time."

Just as traveling ministers must understand how much the pastor has to deal with, pastors need to understand how tough it can be for the traveling minister to schedule their calendar while they wait eternally (weeks and sometimes months) for a response from the pastor that invited them to come. Pastors sometimes meet traveling ministers and say, "I want to have you at my church. When could you come?" They might discuss a few options and the pastor says, "We'll definitely do it. I'll be in touch." You know the rest of the story. There isn't a rest of the story, because the pastor was lying.

Lying is still a sin. It is a pledge of allegiance to Satan, the father of lies. We have taught our children that the *most* dishonorable thing they could ever do is to lie to us. Christians, especially preachers, ought never practice something so devilish. Yet they sometimes do.

"Call me if you're going to be in the area" often means "You can try, but you'll never hear back from me." I don't mean to be negative, but this is so widespread, and people seem to think nothing of it. If an honorable person is nothing else, he or she is a person of their word.

Pastor, if you don't really mean it, please don't say, "I think those dates will work. Give me just a little while, and I'll get back to you." Realize that by the time you finally say "no", the traveling minister is likely not able to book himself anywhere else. That can mean no income for that week, and is a huge lack of consideration.

Sometimes pastors feel that they must cancel a meeting that had already been booked with a traveling minister. Be careful to act honorably. Honor is closely associated with the love of God, and one characteristic of divine love is that it will not hurt the other person, no matter the cost.

Love does no wrong to a neighbor; therefore love is the fulfilling of the law.

Romans 13:10

If a cancelation is absolutely necessary, be sure the minister hasn't already paid for travel. If he has, make arrangements to reimburse him. If it's too late for the guest minister to book anywhere else, send an honorarium. Be honorable in this area and you'll reap honor's rewards.

MISTAKE #10: TALKING ABOUT THINGS AND PEOPLE THEY SHOULDN'T

Although this point was addressed earlier, it is worthy of repetition. Far too much gossip happens at the dinner table between preachers. I know preachers want to catch up on the status of mutual friends. I understand that there are issues on which the traveling minister may have a good perspective, since he is moving around from church to church. These types of things do need to be discussed among ministers, but there are lines that must not be crossed. Gossip and judging are dishonorable, and carry some mighty stiff consequences.

> *Do not speak evil against one another, brothers. The one who speaks against a brother or judges his brother, speaks evil against the law and judges the law. But if you judge the law, you are not a doer of the law but a judge. There is only one lawgiver and judge, he who is able to save and to destroy. But who are you to judge your neighbor?*
>
> *James 4:11-12*

Why do we often act like these verses don't apply to ministers? They do, and it is a grave thing to cast a negative light, or spread dirt about another minister or ministry. The fact is, regardless of how badly a minister has missed it, they still surrendered to God's call at one time. That decision alone is worthy of honor, regardless of whether we agree with their words or deeds. I have decided that my mouth is not going to be the reason another minister doesn't make it in ministry.

Who are you to pass judgment on the servant of another? It is before his own master that he stands or falls. And he will be upheld, for the Lord is able to make him stand.

Romans 14:4

APPENDIX 5

Mistakes The Traveling Minister Makes

MISTAKE #1: FAILING TO HONOR THE PASTOR BEFORE THE PEOPLE

The office of the pastor is the most essential and most familiar ministry office, but one about which many people are ignorant. As a result, pastors are usually taken for granted and under-appreciated. The traveling minister has the opportunity, even with just a few words, to inspire renewed enthusiasm in the people toward their pastor. There is a sense in which every other ministry office exists to support the pastor's office.

While every good minister can be looked at as a hero, this is especially true of the pastor. When I minister in churches, I try to continually show my respect for the pastor's place. For instance, as I am ministering my message, I might say things like, "No doubt your pastor has mentioned some of these things before," or "I can tell you are well taught here." I am not trying to puff up the pastor's ego by showering him with unnecessary praise, I'm just genuinely interested in strengthening the congregation's view of his office. This could be taken to the extreme of course, but subtle references to the greatness of the pastor's role is an appropriate show of honor.

People tend to be overly familiar with their pastor (whom they know), and tend to be over-awed by the guest minister (whom they don't know as well.) There are times when the traveling minister must deflect some of the congregation's affection back to the pastor's office where it rightfully belongs.

MISTAKE #2: SAYING OR DOING THINGS THAT BELONG ONLY TO THE PASTOR'S OFFICE

There are some areas of ministry that belong to the pastor's office alone. For example, establishing the doctrine and beliefs of the local church is the pastor's job. The guest minister's preaching serves to reinforce or amplify what the church already believes. He should not attempt to take the church in an entirely new direction unless the pastor has asked him to do so. For a preacher to usurp the pastor's place by preaching things that are outside the commonly held beliefs of that church is a show of arrogance, pride, and dishonor.

I once had a guest minister speak for us who crossed some of these lines in a minor way (I could see that he was still developing as a minister; he probably wouldn't say the same things today.) What he said wasn't doctrinally incorrect or even untrue, just inappropriate. He was giving his opinion on sensitive and potentially divisive social and political issues. My recommendation to traveling ministers is that they not mention those kinds of things without the pastor's prior permission. Congregations in different parts of the country, or even different parts of town, can have differing views in some of these areas, so these subjects are best left to the pastor.

If the traveling minister does tread upon some of these sensitive areas, the pastor need not be overly concerned. When a pastor has faithfully loved and taught a congregation, that congregation will be extremely loyal to him. I rarely (if ever) found it necessary to bring correction the following week to anything a guest minister said. Bringing correction and clarification to things that *I* had said was a much more frequent occurrence!

But What If I'm Right?

We want to be right about our beliefs. We should all aspire to have sound doctrine and should rightly divide the Word. As important as it is though, being right is not the *most* important thing.

For many years, I appeared on a Christian television show, along with other pastors. The format of this show allowed viewers to call and ask questions about the Bible, and the panel of pastors would take turns answering their questions. There was usually unity among the pastors in their answers, but occasionally one pastor's answer would stray from what I knew the scriptures clearly taught. I would initially become agitated, and would pray for the opportunity to straighten out everyone's thinking!

During one of these times, while I was waiting to unload my *machine gun of the Word*, the Spirit of the Lord spoke to my heart in His still, small voice. I sensed these words rise up within me: "There's something more important than being right." My first thought was to rebuke that voice, as I thought of scriptures like Hosea 4:6:

My people are destroyed for lack of knowledge . . . .

Trust me, if you start quoting scriptures to the Lord to try and prove Him wrong, you will end up being out-quoted.

The next thing I heard was, "The greatest of these is love" (1 Corinthians 13:13.) *Friends, it's more important to apply the law of love than it is to be right all of the time.* The Lord was trying to help me see that if I just tore through a pastor's answer on television, I would make him look bad, possibly bringing harm to his ministry. His people may have been watching, and nothing positive would come from them seeing and hearing another minister trying to prove their pastor wrong.

I learned over time to be diplomatic. I would find any truth I could in the other pastor's answer, and build on it, bringing honor to the minister who said it instead of discounting his ministry. I might begin by saying something like, "My friend, Pastor _____, just talked about the importance of such-and-such, but I'd like to call your attention to another side of this truth." As I learned to always bring honor to my fellow pastors, I noticed that they all seemed to highly respect me. The production staff of that TV station also developed trust in me, and eventually asked me to be the host, calling the shots for the entire show.

MISTAKE #3: INAPPROPRIATE INTERACTION WITH CHURCH MEMBERS

Traveling ministers must remain honorable in their interaction with congregation members. It is not appropriate in most cases for the guest minister to develop personal relationships with people in the churches where they minister. That could negatively affect the people's relationship with their pastor. It is also inappropriate to privately counsel the people. Often, people have already spoken to their pastor and were not satisfied with the answer he gave them. They are looking for second opinions, and are often trying to find a way to justify their unscriptural behavior or decisions.

Many people come right after a service ends to try and speak with the guest minister. Their motives may be pure and their questions genuine. Even so, if the question is about anything other than what I just preached on, I will usually refer them to their pastor. I explain that their pastor is anointed to help them with their life situations in a way that I am not as the traveling minister.

It is never right as a guest minister to trade personal contact information with members of a pastor's congregation without the pastor's prior permission. It is just as wrong for a *pastor* to develop relationships or friendships with members of another pastor's flock. I knew of a very gifted minister who had the habit of staying in contact with some of the members of the churches in which he ministered. This man should have known better, as he was also a pastor himself. Certain pastors found out about this man's activity and asked him to stop, but he refused. This minister, who had one of the strongest healing ministries I have ever known, died prematurely. I believe it is possible that his dishonor toward other pastors, and his inappropriate interaction with members of other churches was the open door that allowed the enemy to work destruction in his life. Remember the story of Eli? Dishonor can cost you your life.

MISTAKE #4: PERSONAL PROPHECIES

Ministers must be careful about the prophetic words from the Lord that they give to church members present in their services. No, we're not against prophecy; in fact, the Word instructs us to earnestly desire the gifts of the Spirit. We simply must be extra certain that we have heard from God before giving a prophetic word to someone. Keep in mind that the pastor of the church is entrusting his most precious asset (his people) to the guest minister.

Prophetic utterance can be very easily influenced by the *soul* of the minister. It is rather easy to say something you see or perceive naturally, all the while thinking you picked it up by the Spirit. If I am in a service and sense the unction to minister to a particular individual, and if the pastor hasn't already made it clear that I have abundant liberty with his congregation, I will stop and ask the pastor if it is okay for me to minister to an individual present. I quickly turn the microphone off, and whisper to him so the people can't hear (and he won't feel obliged to say yes to me.) That is a show of honor toward the pastor's office, and it shows him you respect his place and his people.

An incorrect prophetic word can put someone's life on a wrong course. I know of cases where people have left a church that God had put them in because a minister was casual with prophetic words from the Lord. Ministers must never yield to any perceived pressure to perform. It is never a *must* that spiritual gifts flow in the service. It is a must that we do not leave a mess for the pastor to try and salvage after the meeting is over.

Let's also be careful in this area not to add to what God is really saying. The Bible speaks of *words* of wisdom and *words* of knowledge, but I have heard ministers prophecy paragraph after paragraph of detail to people, most of which was unnecessary. As a usual thing, God is not in the business of revealing every detail of a person's personal life in a public setting. Honor is closely related to respect, and most would agree that it is a matter of love and respect to avoid parading a person's past, troubles, faults, failures, or future before an entire group of people.

> *Whoever **covers** an offense seeks love, but he who **repeats** a matter separates close friends.*
>
> *Proverbs 17:9*

He is not only a God who *reveals*, but He is also a God who *conceals*. Just because we *see* it doesn't mean we are to *say* it.

I traveled with a minister who not only prophesied, but was one of the major prophets in our land. From time-to-time, he would give personal prophetic words to people, but he always included this disclaimer: "I'm human. I can miss it. If what I'm about to say bears witness in your spirit, fine. If it doesn't agree with what's in your own heart, just forget it." I find that statement to be a tremendous show of wisdom, humility, and honor.

MISTAKE #5: OVEREMPHASIZING THE PRODUCT TABLE

Traveling ministers are usually at a church for a relatively short time. That can be frustrating for the traveling minister, because he would like to share his entire ministry with the congregation. Obviously, that can't happen in just a day, or even a week or two. One way the traveling minister can make his revelation and anointing continually available to the people is by offering ministry products during the meeting.

Whether they are sold or given away, there is a degree of caution that must be exercised. The traveling minister is still a guest in that church and must act like a guest. If I am a guest in someone's house, I don't make myself at home unless I am invited to do so. I don't rearrange their furniture to my liking, nor do I start taking things out of their refrigerator.

As a guest in a church, I don't assume that it's okay to set up a product table. I ask permission. Why should I do that? It's good manners for one thing. Also, I understand that just because the pastor was kind enough to allow me to preach doesn't mean he is familiar with *everything* I preach. One error-laced teaching series on someone's table could do more harm over the long-term than what that minister said during the service. If I sense the pastor is not comfortable with my ministry product (that's rarely been the case), I don't push the issue.

Also, I don't promote the product from the pulpit without the pastor's permission. Some ministers spend an excessive amount of time in the service talking about every item on their table. The pastor didn't have you in for that.

As a traveling minister, I have ministry products, all of which are very precious to me. I believe each one contains a strong anointing and would help many. I know my motives are pure, and I want to let people know about what I have been led to produce, but I also must consider the pastor's perspective. It can look like the traveling minister is just trying to market his product, taking more money from the people. Whether that's the case, it hurts no one and helps everyone to spend only a minimal amount of time letting people know about your product table.

Better yet is when the pastor also lets the people know. As a pastor, I would encourage our people to load up on our guest minister's items. I wasn't threatened by their ministry, I valued it. I knew our guest ministers well and had confidence that none of their materials would lead the people astray.

Mistake #6: Fundraising and Gimmicks

If there's not a good anointing on a product, I don't bring it or sell it. When I'm on the road, I'm not a salesman or businessman, I'm a minister. Some traveling ministers carry the equivalent of a Christian gift shop with them on the road, selling every kind of novelty item imaginable. If it's something you were led to do, and it carries the anointing, fine, but otherwise get rid of it. Pastors hate merchandising, because when people succumb to the impulse-buy, the church's offerings usually end up suffering.

Also, traveling ministers should not get up and begin raising funds for their ministry projects, new airplane, new building, etc. without the pastors prior permission. I keep inserting the word *prior* because there have been times when I have seen the guest minister ask the pastor for permission to do something *from the pulpit, over the microphone.* How is the pastor supposed to say no to that? That is manipulation and dishonor. The spiritually immature members of his congregation will think that their pastor is quenching the Spirit if they deny the guest minister's request.

There are still ministers and ministries who make ridiculous promises in exchange for an ultra-sacrificial gift from Christians. Anointed scarlet threads, miracle water, sand from Israel, and other *supernatural debt-busting secrets* are still around today, and need to go away. Any pastor who experiences such nonsense from a guest minister would be right to follow Jesus' example of driving the money-changers from the Temple, and drive that minister out of the pulpit and to the airport for the next flight out of town. It is a show of immaturity, unbelief, ungodliness, and the highest show of disrespect and dishonor for any traveling minister to do anything to funnel money from the people of a church to themselves or their ministry.

MISTAKE #7: PUSHING PARTNERSHIP

Ministry partnership is an interesting (and often combustible) subject. Every minister, whether in a pastoral or traveling role, has more vision than he or she has resources on-hand. That's not a bad thing, it's part of living by faith. One of the ways a traveling minister can do more is by having ministry partners: those who join him with their faith, prayers, and finances. Partnership is a scriptural concept; however, there are ways to pursue partners that are not as honorable as others.

First, I don't believe that every traveling ministry needs a base of partners. When I was called to leave my pastoral ministry and travel, I had no intentions where partners were concerned; the Lord hadn't yet talked to me about that. Then, one day on an airplane, He did. He spoke to me by His Spirit, saying He was calling people to help me, especially so I could get to the places that couldn't normally afford to bring me in. I have a partnership area on my website for that reason alone.

I do not normally mention anything about partnership in the churches where I minister. If I have an established relationship with a particular church or pastor, and was invited to mention it, I would, but otherwise I don't. Having pastored for many years, I realize this: most people in churches don't even tithe. Partnering with my ministry is not something they need to do until they are tithing to their local church.

My spiritual father, Rev. Kenneth E. Hagin, used to say, "It's more important that the local church go on than any other ministry." I completely agree. The local church needs to be funded *first*. People are easily enamored with other ministries and will begin to support them before they properly take care of their own church and pastor.

Brother Hagin also used to say, "I say as little as I can about money." That statement must be clarified. He was making reference to his ministry on the road, not in the churches he pastored. (He actually got in trouble with the Lord for *not* teaching enough about money when he pastored.) Pastors need to say plenty about money to their congregations. Traveling ministers are smart to follow Brother Hagin's example and not emphasize money for their own ministry in the local churches. Believe God for your partners and finances. If honor is in place, He can bring it to you. If honor is not in place, He cannot.

This brings up another interesting point. Many years ago, I was instructed by the Lord to preach biblical prosperity, and to preach it strong. I did so as often as I was led in the church that I pastored, but if I'm led to preach on that subject in a road meeting, guess what I do? I ask the pastor if he's okay with it. Maybe money shouldn't be the sensitive issue that it is in churches, but as long as it remains so, ministers must go overboard to show respect and honor.

MISTAKE #8: SOLICITING NAMES FOR MAILING LISTS

Again, traveling ministers must show honor for the pastor of the church they are visiting. You are a guest, and in no way is your place of ministry equal to the pastor's in *his* church. What's wrong with collecting contact information of interested people in a church? I suppose nothing if the pastor is agreeable to it. Plenty is wrong if it is done without permission. From the traveling minister's perspective, he should think of the people as belonging to that pastor, like a young daughter belongs to her daddy.

When people purchase products from me at my meetings, I often return home with a stack of checks, full of the names, addresses, and phone numbers of church members. Many ministries collect that information, add the names to their mailing lists, and solicit funds from those individuals. I consider that to be inappropriate, and a breach of trust. I do cash all the checks I receive. I do not keep the people's personal information.

We live in the information age, where it is extremely easy for people to find a person or ministry on their own. Let people seek your ministry out. Don't seek them out. Without meaning to, you can discourage their loyalty to their pastor.

My purpose in writing these things is to try and practically illustrate how honor plays itself out in ministry settings. The word *honor* can be an ambiguous term to some, and the concept is one that requires much definition. Hopefully, we have given some clear examples of how honor thinks, talks, and acts. Ministers who take the *bull-in-a-china-shop* approach will struggle in ministry and will lose more friends than they make. Ministers who are honorable can rest in these words of the Master:

> *If anyone serves Me (*"serve" in the Greek is the same as the word "minister"*), he must continue to follow Me [to cleave steadfastly to Me, **conform wholly to My example in living** and, if need be, in dying] and wherever I am, there will My servant be also. **If anyone serves Me, the Father will honor him**.*
>
> John 12:26 (AMP)

About The Author

Faith in God's Word, and continual reliance on the Holy Spirit have been the keys to success in the life and ministry of Rev. Joel Siegel. Raised and educated as a Jew, Joel Siegel, at age 18, had a life-transforming encounter with Christ that brought him true purpose and fulfillment.

Rev. Joel Siegel began preaching and teaching the Word of God soon after he was saved in 1986. He entered full-time ministry in 1990, serving for three years as the music director for the acclaimed gospel music group *Truth*. Truth's road schedule took Joel and his wife Amy worldwide to over 300 cities a year, ministering in churches and on college campuses.

From 1993 to 2000, Joel was the musical director for Rev. Kenneth E. Hagin's *RHEMA Singers & Band*. In addition to assisting Rev. Hagin in his crusade meetings, he produced eight music CD's for the ministry, including his first solo release, *Trust & Obey*.

From 2000 to 2011, Joel and Amy (herself a skilled pastor and worship leader), served as the founding pastors of Good News Family Church in Orchard Park, NY. During this time, they were frequently asked to host shows for the TCT Christian Television Network. Joel regularly hosted their popular *Ask The Pastor* program.

Rev. Joel Siegel spends his time ministering to congregations in the US and abroad, passionately endeavoring to fulfill his assignment to help lead this generation into the move of God that will usher in the return of Christ.

The Siegel's make their home in Colorado. Joel oversees Faith Church Colorado in the town of Castle Rock, where Amy is lead pastor.

For music recordings, audio teaching series, books, and other resources by Joel Siegel, please visit www.biggodmedia.com.

To invite Rev. Joel Siegel to minister at a church or event, please visit www.joelsiegel.org.